# EUROPEAN

# TECHNOLOGICAL

# COLLABORATION

D0610518

# CHATHAM HOUSE PAPERS

General Series Editor: William Wallace
West European Programme Director: Helen Wallace

Chatham House Papers are short monographs on current policy problems which have been commissioned by the Royal Institute of International Affairs. In preparing the paper, authors are advised by a study group of experts convened by the RIIA. Publication of the paper by the Institute indicates its standing as an authoritative contribution to the public debate.

The Royal Institute of International Affairs is an independent body which promotes the rigorous study of international questions and does not express opinions of its own. The opinions expressed in this publication are the responsibility of the authors.

CHATHAM HOUSE PAPERS · 36

# EUROPEAN

# TECHNOLOGICAL

# COLLABORATION

## Margaret Sharp and Claire Shearman

The Royal Institute of International Affairs

Routledge & Kegan Paul
London, New York and Andover

First published 1987
by Routledge & Kegan Paul Ltd
11 New Fetter Lane, London EC4P 4EE
29 West 35th Street, New York, NY 10001, USA, and
North Way, Andover, Hants SP10 5BE

Reproduced from copy supplied by
Stephen Austin and Sons Ltd
Printed in Great Britain by
Redwood Burn Limited
Trowbridge, Wiltshire

Library of Congress Cataloging-in-Publication Data

Sharp, Margaret, 1938-
    European technological collaboration.

    (Chatham House papers, ISSN 0143-5795 ; 36)
    Bibliography: p.
    1. Technology – Europe.    2. Technology –
International cooperation.    I. Shearman, Claire,
1956-   .II. Title.    III. Series: Chatham House
papers ; no. 36.
T26.A1S38   1987    338.9406    86-29798

ISBN 0-7102-1212-7

# CONTENTS

# PREFACE

The Royal Institute of International Affairs undertook this study as a contribution to the important debate about the future of Europe's high-technology industries. It is a central aim of our West European Programme to promote informed discussion among policy-makers, the business and financial communities, and independent experts on a range of issues which concern the political and economic resilience of Western Europe. In this task we owe much to the generous support of the Gatsby Charitable Foundation for the programme as a whole and to the Foreign and Commonwealth Office for facilitating this particular project. In the course of preparing the paper we had the further benefit of much advice and encouragement from a study group of policy-makers, business people, financial experts and academics from Britain and other European countries. Officials of the Commission of the European Communities also helped greatly with their careful explanations of the main research-and-development programmes for which they are responsible. The paper takes account of these various contributions, but of course the authors and I take responsibility for the judgments reached. We all owe a great debt of gratitude to Nigel Pearce for his thoroughness and good-humoured patience in grappling with a text which underwent innumerable modifications, and to Marie Lathia for her speed and accuracy in processing the document.

*February 1987*                                                   H.W.

# SUMMARY

Competitiveness in high-technology industries is widely recognized as being vital to the economies of the developed world. For Europeans, the drive to become competitive has been fraught with problems, especially in such key sectors as information technology and telecommunications. Increasingly, collaboration has been identified as one of several means of improving technological competitiveness. This paper addresses the question of whether and how far European governments should seek actively to promote technological collaboration within Europe.

Chapter 1 explains how competition in high technology has been sharpening, as product cycles shorten, development costs and risks escalate, and technologies converge. Collaboration in various forms has increasingly emerged as a mechanism for sharing costs and matching complementary assets. But these 'strategic alliances' have often been between individual, nationally based European firms and American or Japanese partners, and have not been especially Europe-oriented. Particular characteristics of Western Europe, including the fragmented market, national procurement and regulatory policies, and nationalistic habits, have further inhibited intra-European alliances. Even so, in some sectors, such as pharmaceuticals, European firms have performed well at the global level.

Chapter 2 examines the experiments in collaboration which began in the 1960s. Within the European Community repeated efforts were made to diagnose European weaknesses in technology and to suggest remedies. Given the reluctance of governments and many firms to accept the prescriptions put forward, these efforts bore sparse fruit, as is shown by the experience of Euratom and attempts in other frameworks to develop joint nuclear reactors. However, the catalytic role of the EC should not be underestimated, nor the modest successes in scientific cooperation. In aviation and space, for example, the bedrock of European collaboration was laid in the Airbus project and the European Space Agency. In both these sectors industrialists and governments have been closely involved and practical experience has accumulated.

Chapter 3 explores the resurgence of interest in the 1980s in collaboration through the European Community. The Esprit initiative, originally promoted by Vicomte Davignon, won acceptance as a collective European effort to promote a more effective information technology industry, in contrast to the disparate national programmes and the disappointments of Unidata. The Esprit model has been important in demonstrating to the sceptical that collaboration in R&D can be made to work. It has been followed by sectoral programmes in telecommunications (notably Race) and biotechnology. Cross-sectoral initiatives have been set up to help manufacturers (Brite), to improve the flow of skilled labour (Comett) and to encourage projects in less developed regions (Star). But what can be achieved is severely restrained by resources and the budget wrangles over the EC's Framework Programme.

Chapter 4 sketches the wider context. The European Commission continues to promote the idea of a European Technology Community. European governments have also taken advantage, alongside the EC, of the broader and loosely defined Eureka framework, which is based on a French proposal of April 1985. It is too early to judge the substantive results of Eureka, and especially the aim of improving market-oriented collaboration, but industrialists are becoming increasingly attracted to experiments in collaboration. An important requirement is access to funds for risky and expensive investment in high technology. The habits of private financiers are beginning to change, as the development of the European Venture Capital Association shows. Nevertheless, more can be done to promote the constructive engagement of private capital.

Chapter 5 concludes that collaboration does often make sense, as long as real complementarity can be established among the partners. Other arguments that weight the balance in favour of intra-European collaboration are the dangers of general technological dependency on the USA or Japan, the need for indigenous capabilities in strategic sectors, and worries about US extraterritoriality policies. There are further benefits to be gained from European collaboration in terms of information flows, R&D capabilities and resistance to US and Japanese protectionism. But other policies are needed at the same time: the liberalization of the internal market, tough competition rules and measures to diffuse the results of collaborative research throughout the economy. Collaboration should not be a pretext for cartelization or for pumping money into inefficient operations.

The UK's position is worse than that of many other West European countries. Collaboration in Europe and the other recommendations put forward in this paper all have their part to play in helping British firms in high technology to perform better, but they need to be accompanied by appropriately focused and stimulating domestic industrial policies.

# ABBREVIATIONS

| | |
|---|---|
| ASIC | Application Specific Integrated Circuit |
| AT&T | American Telephone and Telegraph |
| BAe | British Aerospace |
| Bap | Biotechnology Action Programme |
| Bep | Biomolecular Engineering Programme |
| Biceps | Bio-informatics Collaborative European Programme |
| Brite | Basic Research in Industrial Technologies for Europe |
| CAD | Computer-Aided Design |
| CAM | Computer-Aided Manufacture |
| CCITT | Comité Consultatif International Télégraphique et Téléphonique |
| CEGB | Central Electricity Generating Board |
| CEN/CENELEC | Comité Européen de Normalisation/ Electrotechnique |
| CEPT | Conférence Européenne des Administrations des Postes et des Télécommunications |
| CNC | Computer Numerical(ly) Control(led) |
| COCOM | Coordinating Committee for East-West Trade Policy |
| Comett | Community in Education and Training for Technology |
| COST | European Cooperation in the Field of Scientific and Technical Research |

| | |
|---|---|
| CPU | Central Processing Unit |
| Cube | Concertation Unit for Biotechnology in Europe |
| DG | Directorate-General |
| Debene | Deutschland-Belgium-Netherlands |
| EC | European Community |
| ECSC | European Coal and Steel Community |
| ecu | European Currency Unit |
| EEC | European Economic Community |
| EFTA | European Free Trade Association |
| EIB | European Investment Bank |
| ELDO | European Launcher Development Organization |
| ESA | European Space Agency |
| Esprit | European Strategic Programme for Research and Development in Information Technology |
| ESRO | European Space Research Organization |
| ES2 | European Silicon Structures |
| ETC | European Technology Community |
| Eureka | European Research Coordinating Agency |
| Euratom | European Atomic Energy Community |
| EVCA | European Venture Capital Association |
| Fast | Forecasting and Assessment in Science and Technology |
| GATT | General Agreement on Tariffs and Trade |
| GDP | Gross Domestic Product |
| GEC | General Electric Company |
| IBCN | Integrated Broadband Communications Network |
| IBM | International Business Machines |
| ICL | International Computers Limited |
| IKBS | Intelligent Knowledge-Based System(s) |
| ISDN | Integrated Services Digital Network |
| ISO | International Standards Organization |
| IT | Information Technology |
| JET | Joint European Torus |
| mecus | Millions of European Currency Units |
| MITI | Ministry of International Trade and Industry (Japan) |
| NEC | Nippon Electric Company |
| OECD | Organization for Economic Cooperation and Development |

*Abbreviations*

| | |
|---|---|
| OSI | Open Systems Interconnection |
| PC | Personal Computer |
| PTT | Postes Télégraphes Téléphones |
| Race | Research and Development in Advanced Communications Technologies for Europe |
| R&D | Research and Development |
| Rare | Associated Network for European Research |
| RAM | Random Access Memory |
| SDI | Strategic Defense Initiative |
| SMEs | Small and Medium-sized Enterprises |
| Star | Special Telecommunications Action for Regional Development |
| VHSIC | Very High Speed Integrated Circuits |
| VLSI | Very Large-Scale Integration |

# 1

# COMPETITION AND COLLABORATION IN HIGH TECHNOLOGY

Western Europe is not a single economic entity. Yet European governments and companies find themselves operating in an international economy marked by intense competition from the USA and Japan. These two countries have large domestic markets and impressive technological capabilities. They outperform Europe in a number of key sectors of technology. Within Western Europe some important mechanisms exist for fostering economic integration and industrial collaboration, not least in several fields of advanced technology. Foremost among these is, of course, the European Community (EC), which in the thirty-seven years since the Schuman Plan has established itself as the most important framework for collective action. As we shall see later, the EC has embraced some fields of technology as well as creating some of the features of an economically integrated unit. But it still lacks the all-round economic and industrial instruments from which the USA and Japan can benefit in harnessing their technological assets. Alongside the EC, Western Europe has other mechanisms which affect important technological sectors. Just to take two examples, NATO's Independent European Programme Group has focused efforts to increase collaboration in defence procurement; and the European Space Agency (ESA) now has an impressive track record in promoting collective and, in the case of Ariane, internationally competitive products.

Over the past five years or so European technological collaboration has emerged as a core issue on the agenda of both governments

1

and companies in Western Europe. After a difficult and uneasy start, a rash of EC programmes is now under way to promote and increase technological collaboration from the scientific invention through to the product in the market-place. EC policy-makers have the authority, and are beginning to use it more, to create the market conditions which will help European technological industries flourish. Tariff alignment was achieved long ago, but competition rules, market liberalization, and fiscal and legal harmonization are all being pursued on a concerted basis, albeit rather slowly thus far. Around and beyond the EC framework many other activities are under way, some at the company level, some among a small group of countries (Airbus being the leading example), some sectoral (such as ESA), and others operating across Western Europe, like the recent Eureka initiative.

This paper addresses the case for intensifying European technological collaboration in the light of Europe's track record to date, the pressures of international markets and the interconnections between civilian technology and other areas of common European endeavour in the economic, political and security fields. The primary focus is on civilian technology at the point where it begins to generate commercially marketable products. The paper does not therefore discuss, except in passing, scientific collaboration or deal with military technology in any detail, though both areas are of course very pertinent. Rather, it recognizes and explores the tensions between the drive to improve European collaboration generally and the individual cases in which a European company or government may see much merit in preferring an American or Japanese partner. Of crucial importance is the access European purchasers have to good quality, competitively priced technology products, the use of which will enable them to be more effective in their own operations. The debate about European technological collaboration is thus of central importance to governments, companies and societies throughout Western Europe.

The past ten years have witnessed a spectacular growth in collaboration agreements. Indeed, as the OECD describes it, 'the growth in international, inter-firm technical cooperation agreements represents one of the most important novel developments of the first half of the 1980s'.[1] The reasons for this growth are manifold: the fast pace of technological change and the need for a broadened base of scientific and technical resources; the resultant high costs and high risks of investment; the convergence of technologies and the need to have capabilities in many different areas; deregulation, which in turn sharpens the edge of competition; and the need to gain access to markets in the face of worldwide competition.

In some respects, European firms and governments have been slow to recognize the advantages to be gained from collaboration. Public procurement in defence and telecommunications, and separate national standards and regulations, may have kept large sections of the electronics market safe for national champions, but this very fragmentation has weakened the competitive edge of European firms and made markets more vulnerable to competition from the United States and Japan. As much as anything else, it is the incursions already made by these foreign firms into European markets and the fear of further incursion that has led firms such as Philips, Siemens and Thomson to look for partners.

## What do we mean by technological collaboration?

The concept of technological collaboration is broad, ranging from university-based research to joint production agreements between firms, sometimes involving governments. It excludes, on the one hand, collaboration which becomes *de facto* acquisition or merger and, on the other, cooperative agreements relating only to marketing, without any exchange of technology. The spectrum covers:

*Pre-competitive R&D cooperation*
– University-based cooperative research, whether financed by governments or firms or both: e.g. EMBL (European Molecular Biology Laboratory), Heidelberg.
– Government/industry cooperative R&D programmes with university and public research institute involvement: e.g. Esprit.
– R&D corporations run on a private joint venture basis: e.g. the Siemens/ICL/Bull Research Laboratory at Munich.
– Corporate venture capital put up by several firms and invested in one small, high-tech firm: e.g. European Silicon Structures (ES2).

*Competitive R&D cooperation*
– Non-equity cooperative R&D agreements between two firms in selected areas: e.g. the Siemens/Philips semiconductor megaproject.
– Technical agreements between firms concerning completed tech-

nology, including technology-sharing agreements, complex two-way licensing and cross-licensing in separate product markets: e.g. the ICL-Fujitsu link in computers.
– Comprehensive R&D, manufacturing and marketing consortia and joint ventures with or without governmental involvement: e.g. Airbus and the Philips/AT&T joint venture respectively.

The dividing line between the pre-competitive and the competitive is fuzzy. Firms may jointly fund what they term 'generic' research, which precedes commercial applications, but try via patent or other means to appropriate that knowledge for themselves for competitive reasons. In practice the distinction is most evident in relation to EEC competition rules. For the purpose of regulating state aids the European Commission has tried to draw a distinction between pre-competitive R&D (basic industrial research), which, subject to clearance with the Commission, can be granted a level of subsidy of 50 per cent or more, and R&D which is nearer the market, for which progressively lower levels of assistance will be approved. There is a similar distinction in EEC rules relating to restrictive agreements. It is recognized that collaboration on pre-competitive R&D is often not caught at all by the prohibitions in the rules. But joint exploitation of the results normally is caught and needs express exemption if it is to be permitted. Since March 1985, a good number of agreements relating to collaborative R&D, to collaborative R&D *combined with* joint exploitation of the results, or to joint exploitation of the results of prior R&D between the same parties, have been automatically exempt under a 'block exemption' regulation.[2]

**The global challenge**
This shift towards technological collaboration reflects current trends in technology and innovation. The history of industrialization is marked by two broad trends: first, the spread of industrialization to more and more of the world's economies; and, second, the gradual move to increasingly science-based industries. The new technologies of the late eighteenth and early nineteenth century were 'tinkering technologies' developed not from scientific principle but from creative trial-and-error engineering.[3] By the end of the nineteenth century, science and precision engineering dominated the new technologies of that era: the production of steel, the rise of the

chemical industry, and precision engineering for the mass production of interchangeable parts for guns, bicycles, sewing machines, etc.

The trend has continued. By the 1930s, the coal-tar chemistry which had dominated the chemical industry looked decidedly *passé* beside the new chemistry of hydrocarbons, which depended upon the understanding of detailed molecular structures, and in turn brought the postwar wealth derived from new man-made fibres, materials and detergents. Radar, radio and electronics looked increasingly to the applications of solid state physics, nuclear power to high energy physics, and so on. Mature industries were those in which the technology was well tried and codified, whose components of a given size and quality were readily available in international markets, and whose production processes were relatively routine. New industries were those in which experiment was still rife and access to the relevant knowledge-base was therefore an important facet of production. As more and more countries pushed into industrialization, so this distinction became more important. The advanced industrialized countries were those capable of maintaining a sufficiently extensive knowledge-base to develop new industries; mature industries, often more labour-intensive, were increasingly seen as the preserve of the newly industrializing countries, where labour cost less. Such, indeed, was the new world economic order envisaged in the early part of the 1970s.

But a number of factors have upset this new world economic order. One is technology itself. Microelectronics and its associated developments in such fields as robotics and data processing have, in some senses, turned the old logic on its head. Until the advent of microelectronics, technology and economics combined to enhance the importance of size. Mass production demanded standardization and long production runs. The more capital-intensive the plant was, the more highly automated but the less flexible it became; once set, controls were expensive and time-consuming to reset. Where the product-mix changed rapidly, production units remained small, and production increasingly shifted offshore to take advantage of low labour costs, particularly in the Far East.

Today, microelectronics is beginning to change all this. The almost infinite flexibility now offered by computer controls makes the highly capital-intensive, automated production line competitive with labour-intensive production, even when a very diverse product-mix is required. Both large- and small-scale batch production have come back into their own; the computer-controlled machining centre can provide a wide variety of machined parts of all shapes and sizes as cheaply as their standardized, mass-produced counterparts. In addition, computer controls can give guarantees on production quality, size and reliability which no man-made product can rival.

These trends in technology have produced a variety of pressures upon the firm: first, to remain in mainstream product areas and to maintain or improve market share has become increasingly expensive as threshold levels of both capital and R&D expenditure have risen; second, the appreciation that wealth comes from shifting towards higher value-added production has brought increasing pressure on R&D budgets; third, new entrants have emerged in high-technology industries, particularly in Japan and the Far East; fourth, this in turn has challenged the economic and technological hegemony of the United States and precipitated a technology race between the USA and Japan, leaving other countries in danger of becoming the also-rans; and fifth, the costs and risks of new investment in the mainstream product markets have risen and encouraged a retreat into niche markets. The semiconductor industry offers an excellent example of these coincident pressures. The costs of development for mainstream memory devices have increased fast since the early 1970s (Table 1.1, in the statistical appendix). Memory chips are easy to design, but difficult to manufacture, because they require the most advanced production technology in order to minimize feature size. They are 'commodity' products because unlike microprocessors, which are designed into a product, in most situations any brand of memory chip can fill a vacant slot on the printed circuit board, and they are thus subject to intense cycles of feast and famine. Many European manufacturers withdrew from the mainstream memory chip market early in the 1970s, because the difficulty of competing 'from behind' with the leading US producers,[4] combined with the volatility of the market, made attempts to maintain a share of the mainstream market unprofitable compared with the profits to be gained from exploiting the specialist niche markets in custom and semi-custom chips.

But the state-of-the-art technology has moved on. Circuit design and fabrication has developed with the memory chip, and it is now difficult to assume a leading position without sizeable investment in such technology. Meanwhile, the strategic importance of this segment of the market has attracted participation from the large, integrated Japanese electrical conglomerates (NEC, Fujitsu, Toshiba, Hitachi). With their vast resources and captive markets they have rapidly moved into a leading position in the industry, challenging the dominance of the US firms. Finally, as technology has moved towards the submicron level, so development costs have increased, while profitable product life has if anything shortened.

Let us sum this up by pointing to the paradox created by new technologies. On the one hand, as in mainstream semiconductor markets, the intensity of competition worldwide is forcing the pace of technological change and pushing competition inexorably to the global level. Only those firms with substantial resources at their disposal are likely to survive. On the other hand, there is the Volvo phenomenon – the ability to escape the full rigours of global competition in mass-production markets by concentrating production on a niche premium market. Indeed, firms a good deal smaller than Volvo can thrive by satisfying such niche markets at either a national or an international level, many of them as subcontractors for the larger, global enterprises.

**Europe's competitiveness in high technology**
To assess how far European firms are holding their own in high-technology areas, we might begin by looking at the resources they devote to R&D compared with the position in Japan and the USA (Table 1.2). First, by all measures the relative share of R&D in the Japanese economy has increased considerably. Second, the USA devotes practically 50 per cent of its R&D to defence (as does the UK), but even so allocates a higher proportion of GDP to civilian R&D than does Western Europe, though a lesser proportion in recent years than Japan. Third, while Western Europe devotes a lesser proportion of GDP to R&D than either the US or Japan, the contrast is particularly marked in terms of industrial R&D, and especially industrial R&D financed from industrial (not public) sources, a particularly significant indicator.

The growth rates of industrially financed R&D over the period 1967–81 highlight the impressive Japanese performance and the US improvement between 1975 and 1981. At the same time, the European performance continued to deteriorate, albeit only slightly (Table 1.3). There are considerable variations between West

European countries (Table 1.4). In particular, industry-financed R&D as a proportion of value added was greater in West Germany and Sweden than in either Japan or the USA. In Germany, Sweden and France, the growth rate of industrially financed R&D between 1967 and 1981 approached 6 per cent per annum – a stark contrast to that of the UK, which failed even to register as much as 1 per cent growth per annum.

Figures on patents, an output measure of competitiveness in high technology, are predictably similar in broad trends (Table 1.5).[5] Again, however, the diversity within Western Europe is considerable. West Germany's share rose while Britain's was almost halved. France gained as well, ending with a share of patents very close to that of the UK; whereas in 1967 the UK had more than twice France's share of patents. Performance by sectors has varied strikingly, Europe's being above average in chemicals and Japan's above average in metals and transport (i.e. cars). The USA has performed especially well in aerospace (Table 1.6). Patent data also help to provide a useful index of revealed technological advantage. Western Europe's patent share as a whole may be falling, but its technological strengths in the chemicals and mechanical engineering sectors stand out in comparison with both the USA and Japan, while its relative weakness lies in the electrical and electronics area – computing, electrical machinery, radio and television, electrical components and telecommunications. Europe also outdistances both Japan and the USA in two other high-tech sectors – aircraft and nuclear reactors (Table 1.7).

The evidence implies that although Western Europe as a whole does not seem to be pulling its weight in high technology, the problem is essentially one of countries and sectors. Above all, the UK is failing to maintain its position, whereas other countries – particularly West Germany, Sweden and France – have a far better record. Again, reflecting West Germany's strengths, the chemical (including pharmaceutical) and mechanical and heavy electrical engineering industries are holding their own; the big lacuna, and one not to be dismissed lightly, is in information technology.

The same message comes through from the trade statistics. For the period 1965–84 comparative export shares in high-technology products reveal the startling rise of Japan from an export share in 1965 of only 7.3 per cent to over 20 per cent in 1984 (Table 1.8). Among the inevitable losers the biggest is the UK. Until 1980 both

France and West Germany more or less held their own, with France marginally increasing its share, while West Germany's share declined. However, since 1980, both countries have lost export share, whereas the USA, whose decline between 1965 and 1980 was similar to that of the UK, has markedly improved its performance in the past seven years. The USA is also a major importer of high-tech products, with significant Japanese penetration since 1981. Recent trade statistics by sector mirror the technological advantage figures to an uncanny degree. Putting France, West Germany and the UK together, Western Europe's strengths (where they outdistance both the USA and Japan) lie in chemicals and drugs, plastics and heavy electrical machinery; its areas of comparative weakness are in radio and TV, office equipment and computing machines, and communications equipment (Table 1.9).

The degree to which firms pick up and use new ideas in new products or new processes is critical to the process of innovation. One assessment looks at six areas of significant innovation and uses case study material to rank the response in the USA, Japan and Western Europe, and, within Western Europe, to pick out those countries in which there has been a strong positive response from those whose response has been weak (Table 1.10). This confirms Western Europe's comparative advantage in the pharmaceuticals field, and its comparatively poor performance in integrated circuits. Significantly, in two important areas of electronics – robots and software – the European performance ranks second respectively to Japan (in robots) and the USA (in software). In computer-controlled machine tools, in which Japanese firms hold the lead, Western Europe ranks equal second with the USA.

Finally, data on the output of scientific publications reflect the relative strength of basic science, the seed corn from which patents, technological advantage and trade ultimately derive. What is happening to scientific publications today will be reflected in trade statistics in ten to twenty years' time. A recent study shows the growing strengths of Japan, but largely at the expense of the USA, with Western Europe as a whole holding its own (Table 1.11).[6] Within Western Europe, West Germany has been the gainer while Britain and, to a lesser extent, France have been the losers. In citations, which pinpoint the more important publications, Japan's increase has been spectacular, while Britain's traditional strength has been eroded, in marked contrast to France and West Germany.

9

Relative rates of growth in the proportion of scientific studies published can be translated into indices of revealed technological advantage, thereby enabling performance in different scientific fields to be evaluated. Only in three areas – clinical medicine, biomedical research and mathematics – does Western Europe show a relative gain, and only in medicine does it have an advantage over the USA (Table 1.12).

## Is there a technology gap?

The theme of the technology gap is nevertheless one that has re-emerged in Western Europe in the past five years, having been laid to rest in its previous incarnation only in the 1970s.[7] The new technology gap, it is argued, emerged in the 1970s while Europe struggled to respond to the energy crisis and to changing patterns of demand. American companies, with a more flexible labour market, a different investment culture and more innovative business practices, forged ahead, pushing forward the frontier of new technologies and, in their wake, picking up and applying these new technologies in many and diverse fields of activity. Meanwhile Japanese industry adjusted rapidly to the energy crisis and set its sights, through the MITI-inspired VLSI (very large-scale integration) programme, on catching up with US competence in microelectronics. In semiconductors, for example, having had virtually no presence in international markets in the early 1970s, the leading Japanese firms were among the industry leaders by the end of the decade. And, by 1985, NEC displaced Texas Instruments as the main producer of commodity memory chips.

By the early 1980s many European firms (and governments) realized that important developments in such fields as microelectronics and biotechnology had seemingly passed Europe by. Early expertise, acquired from the Americans in the 1960s in areas such as computer-aided design (CAD) or computer numerically controlled (CNC) machine tools, seemed to count for little as the US 'big-league' companies swept through European markets leaving the 'little-league' European firms unable to compete with the breadth or depth of their product range.[8] Likewise, even the expertise of the West German machine tool industry was swept to one side with the invasion of traditional machine tool markets by the Japanese with their automated lathes and machining centres.[9]

Yet the picture is by no means as bleak as some prophets of doom would make out. The solid achievements of the West German chemical and mechanical engineering industries cannot be cast aside lightly; they underpin continuing European strengths in these areas. Take, for example, the ability of the West German machine tool industry to tackle the Japanese challenge head-on, and to come back with a product range that meets and outdoes the Japanese competition.[10] Or take the French expertise in software systems, which is now outdistancing all comers.[11] A broad view across all the data presented in the previous section would appear to reveal two big problem areas: the UK, whose relative decline in both economic and technology terms shows no sign of abating; and the electronics and information technology sectors.

**The roots of Europe's weakness**
The problem is that electronics and information technology provide the central thrust of current developments in high technology. As Chapter 2 shows, although European governments, in the face of a major competitive challenge, managed 'to get their act together' reasonably successfully in the aerospace and space sectors, the same has not been true of electronics and telecommunications. In addition, the USA and Japan have the advantage of being single nations with (reasonably) coherent industrial policies, whereas Europe is a diverse collection of nation states.

The American electronics firms have also benefited from two major advantages denied to their European (or Japanese) counterparts: namely free access to the Bell semiconductor patents and know-how,[12] and the backing of defence and space programme money (and markets) in the crucial early phases of development. These two factors go a long way to explain the emergence and thrust of the US electronics industry in the early 1960s.

The importance of the anti-trust environment should not be underrated either. By restraining giants such as AT&T and IBM from operating outside their mainstream product markets, and in particular from becoming component suppliers, 'little league' firms were given the opportunity to develop and expand in a way which was not always available to European companies. Similarly, the US Department of Defense had extensive procurement programmes, and in particular important applications programmes such as CAD and CNC for machine tools. State-of-the-art techniques, costly and uncertain as they frequently are, need markets to encourage their development, and this was precisely the function performed by US military programmes. Even today, when competition – particularly with Japanese firms – provides the main thrust in civilian markets, US military programmes in very high speed integrated circuits (VHSIC) and Star Wars are providing an important impetus for 'fifth generation' work on artificial intelligence and parallel processing.[13]

Japan's push into electronics did not come until the 1970s and the VLSI programme, which helped raise the sights of companies previously engaged in producing microchips, computers, copiers and office machinery. The role of MITI in coordinating activities, and raising awareness and aspirations should not be underestimated; but nor should it be overemphasized. The sums of money at MITI's disposal have been small; its success lies in having persuaded Japanese companies to commit resources into new product development and to carve out new markets for themselves. But such success could not have been achieved without firms such as NEC (Nippon Electric Company) setting their sights high and being determined to achieve their ambitions.[14]

Why should Europe have failed to seize the opportunities which Japan grasped so readily? There is no doubt that Europe's slow growth throughout the 1970s (and 1980s) has been a contributory factor. Markets have not been growing as fast as elsewhere in the world, and firms in turn have not been encouraged to expand and re-equip, a process which plays a vitally important role in the diffusion of new technologies. Without the spur of competition from Silicon Valley or the Route 128 small firms (which had often grown into large multinationals by the end of the 1970s), Europe's large electronics conglomerates saw no need to change course. Rather, they allowed themselves to become consumed by their own internal problems, often associated with the run-down of their heavy electrical interests, and failed to keep pace with technological developments elsewhere. A good illustration of this is the failure of Siemens to keep up with advances in telecommunications switching, epitomized by their disastrous experience in 1977–8 with EWS-A.[15] In the meantime European markets were penetrated by imports of high-technology products from Japan and the USA.

Fragmentation of the market is the most frequently cited reason for Europe's failings in new technologies. Both critics and apologists of Europe's performance point to the fact that, far from being a common market, in most high-technology products Europe remains a 'Europe des patries', with markets small and fragmented by border controls, other non-tariff barriers and national procurement policies. As a result, it is maintained, no large company within Europe can reap the economies of scale necessary to operate at a global level and thereby hope to compete with US or Japanese firms.

This argument needs careful study. It sounds convincing until it is pointed out that Swedish companies, with a home market base of only eight million people (smaller than Greater London), manage to compete quite well in high-technology markets. ASEA, for example, is Europe's leading maker of robotics, and companies such as Volvo and Electrolux are front runners in the use of robotics and automation in manufacturing processes. Norsk Data, from Norway, is one of Europe's most successful computer firms.

In fact, there are relatively few areas in which the size of the home market is likely to be critical. Aerospace, space and nuclear energy are good examples, and it was early recognition of this which stimulated the collaborative efforts of the 1960s (set out in Chapter 2). In the case of telecommunications similar recognition took much longer. Here the necessary R&D cost of the 1980 generation of switching systems – the first generation of digital systems – needed a minimum investment of $500m, and the new generation expected to be introduced from 1990 onwards has an R&D tag of $1,000m.[16] With the expected life of switching equipment down from 30 years to 10 years, it is reckoned that to justify such an investment a firm must be able to look to sales worth $11,000m per annum, or 8 per cent of the world market. Only two firms in the world (both American) have sales of this size: one is Western Electric, the manufacturing arm of AT&T, which has 17.2 per cent of the market; and the other is ITT (with 11.4 per cent). Of European firms only Ericsson of Sweden (with 6.8 per cent) begins to approach such a market share.

Another area where threshold R&D costs make market size a critical factor is the production of mainstream memory chips: set-up costs for a new wafer fabrication facility have risen to some $200m for a product whose life expectancy has shrunk to two years (Table 1.1). In 1970 the equivalent cost was only $1m and in 1978, Inmos, the semiconductor firm established by the UK government, was set up with an initial investment of $75m and at an overall cost over four years of only $150m.[17] (Within those four years it became one of Europe's largest producers of memory chips and microprocessors, although it has now in fact pulled out of the former.) Such costs were well within the financial ability of firms such as GEC or Siemens, which had cash mountains of $1.5 billion and DM 20.5 billion respectively. Market size *per se* should not, until these past few years, have been the factor inhibiting entry into the semiconductor industry.

Barriers to entry in other areas of information technology (IT) are by no means insuperable, as is evident from the entry (and exit) of many smaller firms in such areas as computers, copiers, software, etc. The convergence of telecommunications and computers has in itself attracted new entrants, as firms such as Olivetti move from typewriters into computers, word processing and now (via its links with AT&T) telecommunications, while AT&T, freed from anti-trust constraints, is moving into the computing and office equipment field. In these cases the concept of the home market is increasingly irrelevant. Small firms may enter specialist segments of the IT market, as LSI Logic did the ASIC (Application Specific Integrated Circuit, i.e., the semi-custom chip) market, but their sales span world markets. To succeed, a firm needs to be competitive world-wide in terms of both price and technology. The more specialized the technology, the higher the premium customers will be prepared to pay. It was the failure of Europe's major electronics giants to focus on competition in world markets that caused the problem.

This turns the fragmentation argument on its head. It is not the small size of the home market *per se* that is the problem, but the fact that many of Europe's electronics firms focused their efforts on home rather than world markets. Why? Because a good part of that home market was protected by one means or another from inter-national competition. Telecommunications provides an obvious example. In all the main European countries, except now the UK, the telecommunications sector is dominated by a public sector PTT, which buys equipment from the private sector electronics firms. Over the years, the need to standardize switching systems and other equipment has led each PTT to establish particularly close relations with a small group of suppliers between whom all orders have been shared. Since it was inconceivable that the public sector PTT would buy equipment from foreign firms, this effectively gave the club suppliers absolute protection in the home market. Purchasers, as well, have often been slow to adapt to new opportunities, thereby depriving producers of the demand pull characteristic of the USA and Japan. In such a position it is all too easy for firms to take the markets for granted and not to bother to upgrade technology when the opportunity arises. If a satisfactory profit can be reaped from sales of existing equipment, why take the trouble to change things? Dang Nguyen, in his study of the European telecommunications industry, criticizes the lack of opportunism of some of Europe's leading equipment makers on precisely these grounds.[18]

But it is not only the telecommunications market that offers scope for opportunism. Two other markets of considerable importance are the defence sector (a major purchaser of electronics equipment in both the UK and France) and the public sector market in data processing equipment. The pursuit of nationalistic purchasing policies in both these markets can mean that as much as 50 per cent of the output of some segments of the electronics industry is effectively removed from international competition. This has a double effect. In the first place it may encourage firms to concentrate on the specialized needs of a limited market-place to the detriment of general sales. For example, military procurement often requires more highly sophisticated technology than the ordinary civilian purchaser requires.[19] In the process, the firm is dragged further away from the international market-place and finds it more and more difficult to compete with its main international rivals, which in turn drives it further into dependence upon protected national markets.

The existence of substantial and protected public sector markets in electronics may therefore take us some way towards an explanation of Europe's deficiencies in IT. Although the USA has pursued policies which are just as nationalistic, the size of the US market is important: its purchases have usually been sufficient to keep at least two, and often more firms in the market, competing with each other. In addition, a much tougher anti-trust legislation, and Pentagon purchasing provisions which guarantee a given percentage share to small companies, have combined to create a generally more competitive environment for high-technology firms. All this underlines the potential benefit to be gained in the EC from the full implementation of a common market in public purchasing.

Nationalistic public purchasing procedures are not the only example of the economic chauvinism that has hindered the competitiveness of European firms. The 1960s and 1970s were the era of the 'national champion', the deliberate attempt on the part of governments to create 'flag-carrying' firms in most important areas of high-technology (namely, computers, aerospace, telecommunications and nuclear power). Such national champion policies also characterized some sectors of the mature industries and services, again constraining the demand side. National champions were partly a response to American import penetration and were fed by Gaullist ambitions to create defence capabilities independent of the USA. They reflected a general belief that big was beautiful, and that the future lay with large firms (such as IBM) which could reap full advantage from economies of scale. National markets, it was argued, could only support one such firm, and, to help accelerate what was seen to be an inevitable move towards concentration, governments actively intervened in the market to 'rationalize' industrial structure. This period was characterized in Britain by the Industrial Reorganization Corporation (IRC) and its marriage-broking activities, and in France by the Plan Calcul and the creation of firms such as CII in computers, Framatome in nuclear power and Thomson in electronics. It has also to be said that in many sectors there was deep resistance to collaboration with sister companies in other European countries, for reasons which had little to do with economic logic.

In France the national champion era was succeeded in the late 1970s by the concept of the *filière* – the idea that a single national flag-carrier was not enough; it needed to be supported by a national capability both upstream and downstream.[20] The *filière électronique*, for example, embraced upstream capabilities in semiconductors and downstream capabilities in telecommunications, computers and consumer electronics. To be competitive in electronics, it was argued, France needed capabilities in all these important 'node' activities, with the upstream activities assuming a particular importance in the early phases of the product cycle. In other words, the concept of the *filière*, applied to a strategic industry such as electronics, argued for across-the-board competence in all mainstream activities in the industry. To be reliant on foreign firms and foreign technology was to capitulate to economic weakness. This approach took the French into difficult debates in the 1980s about whether other Europeans were to be categorized in the same way as the rest of the world.[21]

Although instinctive French economic nationalism went further than that of any other European country, it nevertheless epitomizes the relative economic and technological chauvinism which pervaded European thinking in the 1970s. Europe's shortcomings in information technology reflect two major failures of policy on the part of both firms and governments: the failure to use the breadth of the European market to build up international competitiveness; and the fallacy of thinking that home-grown technology is superior to imported technology. The difficulty is that these failings feed upon each other. The reinforcement of poor technology means difficulties in competing internationally, which lead to pleas for protection, which, if granted, tend to isolate the industry yet further from competition and make it doubly difficult to compete.

**Why collaboration is now on the agenda**
Collaboration has become a worldwide phenomenon in high technology (Tables 1.13 and 1.14). Furthermore, the trend is clearly upwards, with the number of collaborative agreements increasing year by year, especially in the 1980s. The number of intra-European agreements increased in the years 1983–4, although these are still topped by the number of agreements between European and US firms. In four sampled high-technology areas – aeronautics and space; biotechnology; advanced microelectronics and data processing; and new materials – both agreements between European firms and agreements made by European firms with firms in the USA show a clear upward trend (Table 1.13). This increase is evident both in agreements over the exchange of knowledge and in those concerned principally with manufacturing or marketing.

What lies behind this increased interest in collaboration? We have already identified a number of factors – the rising costs and high risks of investment in some of these areas, the convergence of technologies and the need for capabilities which span both scientific disciplines and business experience, and the increasing need to look for global markets. It is worth exploring these in a little more detail.

The high costs, coupled with the high risks of investment in new products such as semiconductors, are forcing many companies to find partners to share the burden of product development, manufacturing and marketing. Companies in new technological areas may also need to pursue several research paths, testing various versions

17

of a product before settling for one specific design. In the aircraft industry, for example, a new commercial aircraft takes five years and up to $2 billion to develop.[22] Companies in the European aerospace industry just do not have the resources to put into such development and therefore have no choice but to look to collaborative deals. Such indeed has been the logic of the European aerospace industry ever since the early 1970s, for the Airbus series, for certain military aircraft developed jointly among the independent European companies, and for a number of arrangements with Japanese or American partners.

The risk of loss has also risen as the increasingly competitive environment has cut product life-cycles. In areas such as micro-computers, a product may find that its next generation is launched within as little as six months of its own. Although this does not necessarily mean that it will no longer sell, it often means a substantial price-cut and the loss of the high profit margin enjoyed by a product when it is ahead of its competitors.

The convergence of technologies is another cause for collaboration. Gone are the days when a company could operate in, say, computers, without having some involvement with local area networks in telecommunications. Similarly, development teams have to be increasingly cross-disciplinary, bringing together skills from many different areas. Few national companies in Europe have sufficient resources to develop all capabilities internally. Acquisitions are costly and difficult to integrate, but collaboration seems to offer a quick and effective way of obtaining the necessary expertise. Olivetti is a good example of a firm that has linked up with others both large and small to transform itself from a typewriter company into one of the world's largest office automation companies. Link-ups with small entrepreneurial firms, such as Acorn, have given it access to new technologies and new products, while the link with AT&T has provided, on the one hand, important expertise in office telecommunications systems and, on the other, access into AT&T's US distribution network for its own office automation products. A recent link-up with Toshiba has provided access to Toshiba's office automation technology and a useful marketing base for its own products in Japan.

Collaboration is a means of obtaining what Teece in a recent paper called 'complementary assets'. As Teece explains, 'in almost all cases the successful commercialization of an innovation requires that the know-how in question be utilized in conjunction with the services of other assets ... In some cases, as when an innovation is systemic, the complementary assets may be other parts of a system. For instance, computer hardware typically requires the development of specialized software, both for the operating system as well as for applications.'[23] The precise key assets needed by firms operating in such a competitive environment will vary from industry to industry and firm to firm. Many collaborative deals between large and small firms often verge on subcontracting: a large established leader in an industry can often impose its terms on smaller partners. Sometimes, however, the small firm may have the whip hand and be able to force the larger firm to give it the major share of the profits.

The search for complementary assets presents some interesting dilemmas when large oligopolistic rivals of more or less equal technological and financial strength are involved. In effect it means collaboration with competitors or potential competitors, and requires complex deals whereby companies agree to cooperate in some areas while simultaneously competing in others. The tie-up between Philips and Siemens in semiconductors is of this type: the two companies, long-term rivals in electrical and electronic engineering, have pooled resources to develop one-megabit and four-megabit memory chips (the so-called megaproject). K. Ohmae, in his book *Triad Power*, claims that such collaboration is becoming a necessary part of business strategy and suggests that the three-way axis – the USA, Japan and Europe – provides a basis for triad power among companies: 'Two bases for decision (about whom to collaborate with) are geography and industry. Consortia allies should not be too close or in your triad region. Distant foes can be close friends, while cousins can be foes. This can be seen in the European transnational mergers (of the 1970s). Most of these mergers failed because they involved links between similar companies, which ended up hating each other. They could not work as partners because they were too close and their businesses too much alike.'[24] Ohmae's view of the strategic 'war games' being played between the major multinationals can be viewed as a simplistic model of current events that ignores the key economic and technical factors which are driving companies towards cooperation. Nevertheless, the concept of strategic alliance is an important one, and helps to explain why collaboration *within Europe*, as distinct from collaboration across the Atlantic or with Japan, has perhaps been less attractive.

But there are a number of factors which have tended to bring European firms together and explain why European technological cooperation has become a live issue. One of these has undoubtedly been the 'Eurosclerosis' debate, which emerged in 1983–4. The *Wall Street Journal* published in January 1984 an assessment typical of the pessimism prevalent at that time. Although it dramatized and exaggerated the degree to which Europe was lagging technologically behind the USA and Japan, nevertheless it focused the attention of businessmen and politicians on Europe's failing competitiveness. As Chapter 3 shows, a variety of EC initiatives had already been launched to stimulate European technology. Accentuated fears about declining competitiveness made the Community level of action much more relevant. The pilot stages of Esprit had had only lukewarm support in 1982, but Vicomte Davignon, the Commissioner for Industry between 1977 and 1984, put his weight behind the full initiative, which began in 1984, and rapidly added to Esprit further initiatives on telecommunications (Race), biotechnology (Bap) and the manufacturing applications of technology (Brite), together with a range of associated cross-sectoral programmes.

These formal EC initiatives were backed by business. The Gyllenhammer group, although led by a Swedish (i.e., non-EC) businessman, brought together the heads of Europe's leading businesses to provide the necessary informal network of support. These business leaders were worried that their companies had fallen behind US and Japanese technology and were anxious to promote steps which strengthened Europe's technological base. They recognized that this meant action on several fronts: strengthening the internal market within Europe itself, encouraging standardization, introducing competition in such areas as public purchasing, and urging Europe's businesses to make full use of the division of labour within Europe. They argued that the greatest danger to Europe's competitiveness lay in the continued fragmentation of the European market. The earlier phase of collaboration in the 1960s had focused mostly on big projects; this new wave of collaborative enthusiasm engaged both governments and industrialists from a wide range of technological sectors in defining the policy instruments and market conditions which were needed to enable European industry to thrive in terms of R&D capabilities and competitive production.

But it was not just late recognition of the momentum of technological innovation that influenced European thinking. The deregulation of AT&T, finally achieved in January 1984, and the more or less simultaneous settlement of the long-standing US anti-trust suit against IBM, provoked a powerful concentration of minds. The former may have broken up Ma Bell in the USA, but it released the US telecommunications giant from the restriction on overseas operations. AT&T, with its vast resources and the technological expertise of the Bell Labs behind it, was all set to become a player on the European scene. IBM was, of course, already a major player, but the settlement of its anti-trust suit gave it the opportunity to move into the telecommunications market, from which it had previously been barred. If IBM began moving into this market in the USA, it was likely to become a major player in Europe as well. Although covert protectionism through such devices as voluntary export restraints might enable European business to duck the Japanese challenge, no such option was available with the American giants – AT&T and IBM. European business had to put its own house in order.

Another event of significance was the dispute with the US administration over contracts for the Soviet gas pipeline, which brought to a head the extraterritoriality issue. Although the Reagan administration had strengthened the COCOM controls over the exports of strategic equipment to the Soviet bloc, it required a major project, such as the pipeline, to demonstrate the full and damaging effect (for Western Europe) of the tight implementation of these controls. It also raised the spectre in Europe of the Americans effectively limiting European access to US technology. Suddenly the realization came that if Europe were forced into a position of dependence upon its own technological resources, it was vital that those resources were adequate. America's new protectionism gave a new logic to the technological protectionism enshrined in French ideas about the *filière*.

Meanwhile, the accumulation of concern about Japanese success was encapsulated in the incident of Poitiers – the declaration of November 1982 from the French administration that all French imports of video-recorders had to be shipped to Poitiers in central France for customs clearance. In itself easy to ridicule, the incident nevertheless marked the high point in the battle in the Socialist administration between the 'introverts' (led by Chevènement) and the 'extroverts'. The eventual recognition that France was an interdependent entity within the Common Market and could not go it alone in terms of either trade or technology shifted the technological debate that had been taking place within France to the European level. From March 1983 onwards the weight of the French government swung sharply behind Davignon's initiatives within the European Commission. Equally important, the Poitiers incident served as a sharp warning to the Japanese that European governments could be driven to uncongenial measures, and reinforced the importance of the EC-Japan dialogue.

In parallel to the increasing support for initiatives to promote technological collaboration in Western Europe, we have seen the increasing salience of moves to liberalize and integrate the European market. The Cockfield programme to establish a single internal market by 1992 gives these moves concrete expression. So also does the increasingly vigorous debate about the other conditions to be met in terms of, for example, more appropriate rules of competition and more effective channels for private as well as public investment in European technology for commercial exploitation.

Beyond these primarily economic factors, we must also recognize the stimulus of the debate on European defence collaboration. The dividing line between civil and military technologies is a fine one and many of the same companies are involved in both kinds of application. Pressure on defence budgets, worries about US technology controls and hegemony, and a more diffuse concern about US intentions over the longer term, have all combined to make the European frame of reference for defence industries a much more serious candidate for attention. Economic logic, technological complementarity and political preferences do not, of course, necessarily point in the same direction, but specific choices about partners for collaboration have to take all of these factors into account, especially when governments as well as companies are involved. The consequent dilemmas for some Europeans were crystallized when the Americans invited Europeans (and others) to participate in the Strategic Defense Initiative. SDI provoked divided and uncertain responses in Western Europe. One consequence was the initially French-led Eureka initiative, which is discussed in Chapter 4. It came to constitute in the end not a European alternative to SDI but another European framework, alongside the EC, for promoting collaborative arrangements in Western Europe in high technology.

Underlying the whole debate about collaboration in high technology, whether with European or other partners, is the tangled question of what constitutes success. Concorde was successful technically, but not commercially. Examples in later chapters will highlight particular cases and the different ways of analysing them. As a preliminary observation suffice it to comment that what is 'successful' depends essentially on the stated objectives of any particular collaborative arrangement. Economic logic generates one set of criteria, commercial considerations may introduce others and the unavoidable intrusion of political or defence arguments may suggest still more. Clarification of the central objective is thus crucial to any judgment about when European partnership may be the best course of action.

# 2

# EARLY EXPERIMENTS IN EUROPEAN COLLABORATION

This chapter reviews the early efforts of the European Community to promote technological collaboration, and considers in more detail a sample of collaborative projects started in the 1960s. The aim is to distil from them lessons which are relevant to the current debate, not to provide comprehensive case histories. The three sectors – nuclear energy, aviation and space – shared certain features which, in the context of the 1960s, made them prime candidates for collaboration and made the European framework seem particularly attractive. First, they were prestige technologies in which governments had strong interests and were primary customers. The pursuit of supersonic transport through Concorde, for example, was even described in one British publication as 'in scale and complexity . . . comparable to the USA's Apollo moon-shot programme'.[1] Second, the early stages of their technological development coincided with a period of global economic growth which facilitated relatively generous public funding, at least initially. Third, in each of the three we can find echoes of the major underlying political themes of the day: that is, the question of European dependence on US technology, the role of the European Communities, and a jostling for position within Western Europe.

Within each sector there were also specific incentives to promote collaboration. Industrialists in the aerospace industry recognized very early on the need for collaborative solutions. The scale and complexities inherent in aerospace developments, both civil and military, were beyond the capabilities of the firms in any one European state. Although a European framework did not emerge for all areas of aviation, it seemed promising for some projects, again both civilian and military. It was a similar story for the space sector, in which from the outset purely national options were recognized as not viable. The potential dangers implicit in nuclear power development militated in favour of international regulation and a collective search for peaceful applications, to which the European framework appeared especially appropriate.

**The role of the European Community**

The concept of economic integration was a major theme in Western Europe during the 1950s. The establishment of the European Coal and Steel Community (ECSC) under the Treaty of Paris in 1951 opened the way for further negotiations among Europe's Six, and led to the formation of two new Communities – the European Economic Community (EEC) and the European Atomic Energy Community (Euratom) – under the Treaties of Rome in 1957.

For all three Communities the 1960s constituted a period of experimentation that naturally extended to the debate over technological collaboration, which logically fell within the integration remit. Views on collaboration were also heavily influenced by the controversy over Europe's technology gap as outlined, for example, by Servan-Schreiber.[2] Essentially based on political interpretations rather than close economic analysis (see Chapter 1), the ensuing debate gave rise to the notion of developing a new technological community within Europe. The Italians, for instance, toyed with the concept of a 'technological Marshall Plan', while the French proposed that the European Commission begin a study of industrial and research policies within the Six.

The question of Britain's membership of the EC was part of the same debate. Britain's own view that its technological expertise constituted its strongest hand was underlined not only by the Commission,[3] but also by a Council of Europe report asserting that to 'be viable it is doubtful whether a European Technological Community could go it alone without the United Kingdom'.[4] With the benefit of hindsight it is somewhat ironic that Britain was perceived to be the cornerstone of such a community, yet at the time it aptly reflected the image of modernization promoted by Britain's

25

Minister for Technology, Tony Benn, and Prime Minister Harold Wilson. Indeed, Wilson believed that his 1967 proposal for 'a drive to create a new technological community' in Europe and his subsequent seven-point plan, put forward at the time when Britain was making its second formal application to join the EC, played a crucial role in convincing the other Europeans that Britain 'meant business'.[5]

Various suggestions were put forward as to the form such a technology community should take. Two of the more influential views emanated from Jean Monnet's Action Committee for a United States of Europe[6] and Christopher Layton's book *European Advanced Technology: A Programme for Integration*.[7] Monnet called for a new institution concerned with technological cooperation to be established in conjunction with the EC Commission, while Layton outlined fifteen policy recommendations ranging from basic science to legal and financial support provisions. His suggestions also included a European merger-promoting agency, common purchasing, industrial Community R&D contracts, a European Advisory Council and a Technology Assessment Centre. Many of these were to be paralleled in the various policy proposals put forward by the European Commission.

### A common approach to industry

Although the ECSC and Euratom treaties conferred specific responsibilities for the coal, steel and nuclear industries upon the Community, no formal provision existed for general industrial or technology policy. What the Treaty of Rome (EEC) did provide, however, was a range of policy powers which could be used to determine the regulatory framework and market conditions for European industry. Thus, competition policy, freedom of capital and labour movements, the right of establishment, customs union, harmonization of national laws, and state aids fell within the treaty's competence. But they were not subsumed under a general framework for industrial policy.

The Commission nevertheless determined to establish some form of industrial policy. Initial attempts focused on steps towards the creation of a single market, but experience soon proved this to be much more difficult than had been anticipated. In July 1967 the Commission established a separate Directorate-General for Industrial Affairs (DG III), and two kinds of policy proposal began to emerge. The first was a response to US market penetration of

Europe, and promoted the idea of transnational mergers and 'European' companies.[8] The second found expression in the Commission's 1970 Memorandum known as the Colonna Report.[9] This called for the elimination of technical barriers to trade and the opening up of public purchasing; the harmonization of European legal, fiscal and financial frameworks; the encouragement of transnational mergers; the need for industrial readjustment and adaptation; and a Community position on multinational corporations.

For Community officials, the going was hard. While DG III promoted European concentration and mergers, DG IV (Competition) brought the latter under closer scrutiny and control. Early discussions revealed sharp disagreements among member states over the Colonna Report's underlying philosophy. German advocacy of a free-market economy clashed with French ideas of interventionist strategies. The Commission's attempts to break the deadlock in April 1971, with a proposal for an Industrial Policy Committee under the joint auspices of the Council of Ministers and the Commission, failed in the face of French opposition to the Commission's role and the Council's preoccupation with the issue of enlargement. Only towards the end of the decade, when the situation facing the steel, ship-building and man-made fibre industries became more critical, was DG III able to start developing an effective role for itself.

*A common technology policy*
The 1967 Memorandum of the Medium-Term Economic Committee led the first Council of Science Ministers to commission a further report in October of that year on six broad technological sectors: transport, oceanography, metallurgy, environmental problems, meteorology, and data processing and telecommunications. Opinions differed on the quality and acceptability of specific proposals, but it is interesting to note the perceptive diagnosis of key problems of data processing and telecommunications. Detailed discussion was delayed by the debate over Britain's application for EC membership and France's refusal to include all four candidate countries. Eventually, in December 1968, the committee resumed its work under the leadership of Pierre Aigrain, French Delegate-General for Scientific and Technical Research. Over forty projects for European-owned companies (to avoid encouraging further US penetration) were put forward under the six sectoral headings already identified. Comments were invited from the four applicants

27

to the Community, together with Switzerland, Sweden, Austria, Spain and Portugal, and later from Finland, Greece, Yugoslavia and Turkey, in recognition of the importance of examining the technological issues in a broad European context. In November 1971 an outline European plan was agreed in the form of COST (European Cooperation in the Field of Scientific and Technical Research), with seven initial projects at a cost of $21.5m. Parallel proposals for a European R&D Committee (CERD) and a European R&D Agency (ERDA) met with little response.

COST has become a useful framework for the preparation and implementation of European projects involving applied scientific research. Each of its nineteen members (i.e., all the European OECD member states and a representative of the Commission) enjoys the same rights whether it is a member of the European Community or not. The EC as an entity also participates in COST actions and projects. COST is not an independent international organization, but rather an international association with jointly determined obligations. For each project, therefore, the form of cooperation is individually negotiated in simple purpose-built agreements. Since its inception the scope of COST has expanded so that its projects now scan ten broad research areas: namely, informatics, telecommunications, transport, oceanography, metallurgy and material science, environmental protection, meteorology, agriculture, food technology, and medical research and health. Further details on some of these are found in Chapter 3.

This brief history of EC efforts demonstrates the early diagnosis of some of the key technological issues facing Western Europe and points up the relevance of collaborative arrangements. The agenda and membership were flexibly defined, but the detailed work did not command a high political profile. Nor could it escape the constraints imposed by a lack of agreement on the overall thrust of industrial policy and by difficulties in opening up the European market.

**The nuclear sector**

*The experience of Euratom*
The experience of the European Atomic Energy Community has been well documented. Its main objective was to encourage the creation and growth of an atomic industry in Europe based on a

broadly conceived common programme of research. Four joint research centres were set up to coordinate pioneering activities in the field – at Karlsruhe (West Germany), Ispra (Italy), Geel (Belgium) and Petten (the Netherlands). Areas of research covered by Euratom agreements included fast breeder reactors, high-temperature gas reactors, nuclear ship propulsion, and nuclear applications in agriculture and medicine. Of these the quest for a joint European reactor was potentially the most important, given expectations of the scope for the development of civil (and peaceful) nuclear power. In addition, Euratom took on important responsibilites for regulating civil nuclear energy and materials and ensuring safeguards (though these are not the primary concern of this paper).

Responses to Euratom's research agenda were initially enthusiastic, but as time went on the problems increased. These hinged on Euratom's financial arrangements. Two five-year research programmes had been agreed on, with initial funding for 1958–62 of £75m, which was doubled for 1963–7. But at the end of the second in December 1967, the development of nuclear power reactors on a Community basis was abandoned following the failure of the member governments to reach a consensus on what was to come next. Attempts to redefine Euratom's research role led to five years of interim annual budgets before a four-year programme was eventually adopted in February 1973. This covered both nuclear and non-nuclear research, with projects ranging from reactor safety and radioactive waste disposal to environmental protection, industrial standards and satellites. The joint research centres meanwhile were reorganized with only Belgium, West Germany and the Netherlands contributing towards Petten, and Italy taking responsibility for the heavy-water test reactor at Ispra. The much later JET programme at Culham, on nuclear fusion, is an interesting example of scientific collaboration, but is as yet a long way from an exploitable process.

For Euratom's research efforts, therefore, the 1960s was a period of continued crisis. As one commentator has noted, its basic problem lay in the fact that, as an organization and set of objectives, it was the product of mistaken assumptions.[10] The predicted fuel shortage in Europe failed to materialize. The novelty and potential of nuclear power ensured the growth of national programmes, and French military interests denied Euratom any effective role. Euratom was an institutional response to R&D needs which quickly became commercially oriented. Power plant firms were in strong competition with each other and preferred to exploit their historic links with US firms. They were also tied to deeply rooted patterns of national procurement, standards and regulation. Members had little incentive to pursue collective projects. Thus Euratom, by its own admission, failed to coordinate its members' activities. The transnational industrial arrangements which were beginning to evolve had little, if anything, to do with Euratom's efforts.

## *The case of fast breeder reactors*[11]

As Euratom's experience so clearly illustrates, interests in nuclear R&D were predominately nationalistic even when pursued within a European framework. For many of the developments in nuclear technology this remained the case, although cooperation in the nuclear fuel cycle through URENCO and Eurodif has been sustained with commercial success. This section focuses on European industrial collaboration in fast breeder reactors, because it usefully illustrates the ways in which attitudes to collaboration alter in response to changing circumstances.

By and large the development of fast breeder reactors in Western Europe has taken place through collaboration, though much of it without British participation. Broadly speaking, this has entailed five distinguishable phases involving a variety of participants from industry, electricity utilities and research centres across five, and latterly six, European countries. The nature and quality of the collaboration has varied over time, but the programmes themselves reflect a broadly incremental progression in terms of their objectives and organization.[12]

The earliest stage of European fast breeder reactor collaboration emerged under Euratom's umbrella, but the results were disappointing. Duplicate programmes were sanctioned in France and Germany, and by 1965 Euratom had also entered into contracts with Italy, Belgium, the Netherlands and Luxembourg. Euratom did, however, serve to foster links between Germany, Belgium and the Netherlands which were to emerge in a more pragmatic form of collaboration outside the European Community.

This second phase of collaboration was known as the Debene (DEutschland-BElgium-NEtherlands) programme. By 1968 the general context for collaboration had altered. Industrial application of fast breeder reactors was now considered imminent and Franco-German competition had become the prime factor behind the technology's development. France withdrew from the Euratom programme to pursue its national one, while Germany, Belgium and the Netherlands signed an intergovernmental agreement to construct a prototype plant, the SNR 300. Costs were allocated on a 70/15/15 per cent basis respectively, with the electricity utilities adding 7.8 per cent to the governmental funding. The industrial division of labour was determined at governmental level. Duplication occurred over fuel fabrication, since the political implications implicit even at the prototype stage precluded any form of German dependence on external sources of fuel supply. Industrial and utility consortia were established, and the British CEGB joined the latter in 1973 with a minority shareholding of 1.65 per cent.

Although the governmental go-ahead for construction of the SNR 300 was given in March 1972, the reactor has still not been completed. The major constraint has been the delays inherent in the German licensing system, which anti-nuclear groups have exploited to good effect to express their opposition. This in turn has led to cost escalations which have finally forced the Belgian and Dutch governments to impose a ceiling on their contributions. The agreed division of finances has had to be renegotiated, and Germany's share has risen to approximately 85 per cent.

Meanwhile, outside of the Debene programme a third phase in European fast breeder reactor collaboration was emerging. For the nuclear sector generally the period from 1968 to 1972 had witnessed a gathering momentum of collaboration at the industrial level. In fast breeder reactors this was reflected in the 1973 agreement between the French, Italian and German utilities on the construction of two industrial power stations, Superphenix in France and SNR 2 in Germany. For each reactor the host utility was to fund 51 per cent of the costs, the Italian utility 33 per cent and the remaining partner the balance. Industrial contracts were to be allocated on a corresponding basis. Since the Debene SNR 300 was still under construction, efforts focused largely on the Superphenix programme. France, having completed its national prototype, Phenix, approached the collaboration from a position of strength. Thus, while the Debene countries hoped primarily to keep up with the technological state-of-the-art, the French also aimed to secure the benefits of reduced costs, more rapid technological development and a wider market. A joint Franco-Italian industrial partnership was established between Novatome (a French firm created specifically for the purpose) and Nira, the success of which led the two firms in 1978 to conclude a long-term collaboration agreement on fast breeder reactor design.

During this third phase of collaboration it proved difficult to maintain the precise national allocation of contracts set up under the utility agreements. France's overall share of the Superphenix contracts was up by about 3 per cent, Italy's by 2 per cent and Germany's down by 5 per cent. The major cause lay in the lack of protection for the transfer of know-how from France and Italy to the Debene countries. The Novatome/Nira cooperation had developed within a well-defined framework of research and industrial agreements between France and Italy. No such facility existed for the Debene countries. The Superphenix collaboration was therefore extended to encompass the Serena framework.[13] This marked the fourth phase of collaboration and facilitated a whole network of fast breeder reactor agreements and exchanges of know-how between France (in partnership with Italy) and Germany (on behalf of the Debene countries).

Progress has been greater on Superphenix than on SNR 2. Designed to follow the SNR 300 (still under construction), the German SNR 2 is still at the preliminary stage. France meanwhile has developed design plans for Superphenix 2. This, together with a combination of economic constraints, technological complexity and receding commercialization prospects, has led to problems in the implementation of the most recent collaboration phase. Changes have also occurred in the collaborative partnership. Britain has entered the scene following its government's decision against further national programmes, while domestic pressures have led to a Dutch withdrawal. The new collaboration was marked by the signing of a Memorandum of Understanding in 1984 for the progressive construction of three 'European' reactors, one each in France, Britain and Germany, over the next three decades. In terms of the reciprocal arrangements in the Superphenix agreement, the German SNR 2 would seem the prime candidate for the first of the new generation, yet Superphenix 1 has actually been built and so French plans for its next model are under way. German participation meanwhile is contingent on the next reactor within these agreements being built in Germany. Unsurprisingly, progress towards implementation of the

1984 Memorandum has been slow, not only because the predicted scarcity of uranium supplies, so much a spur in the early attempts at collaboration, has failed to materialize, but also because of the technological complexity of the reactors.

## The aviation sector

Since the early 1960s the world aircraft market has been subject to the impact of large-scale US civil and defence aerospace programmes. This, together with US advantages in terms of available resources and domestic market size, has increasingly forced European governments and industry to look to collaboration on major aerospace projects. The Franco-German Transall and Atlantic projects of the 1950s marked the first tentative steps down this road, and the Anglo-French Concorde the first attempt at a joint project entailing a really large-scale technical challenge. Experience was consolidated with the Anglo-French helicopter package and Jaguar project, which were successful, and the Anglo-French Variable Geometry combat aircraft, which was not. By the end of the 1960s confidence in European collaboration had increased to the point at which Britain, Germany and Italy could launch the Tornado, which was the first really challenging aircraft project to be undertaken by three as opposed to two partners.

These projects are relevant to this current paper chiefly because of the broader lessons learned from them, lessons which may seem obvious today but were less so at the time. Concorde is important because of the major psychological impact it exercised on British perceptions of European collaboration. When the Anglo-French Treaty was signed in 1962, two types of supersonic aircraft – medium-range (France) and long-range (UK) – had been envisaged. A lack of orders for the former, however, led to a focus on the latter. Both parties were bound by treaty obligations and domestic political considerations. Major redesigns, inadequate financial controls, inflation and devaluation led to cost escalations. Marketing Concorde proved difficult. Only fourteen aircraft were actually produced – seven each for British Airways and Air France – all of which had to be subsidized in terms of both capital and running costs. But the partnership of British Aerospace and Aerospatiale induced a sharpened awareness of the methodology of collaboration which was to prove enormously important in the judgments made subsequently by both industries and government about how to structure successor projects.

### The European Airbus

Perhaps the most relevant single case study among the European collaborative ventures launched in the 1950s and 1960s is that of Airbus Industrie.[14] The concept of a short- to medium-range, wide-bodied airliner originated in Britain and France during the early 1960s. Negotiations between the two governments and industrial contractors were joined by the Germans in 1966. By early 1967 the airframe companies had produced a design outline. Rolls-Royce were to provide the engine design and the French to lead the airframe design. The three governments signed a Memorandum of Understanding in September 1967 to develop the A300 aircraft. The three national airlines were each to buy 25 of the aircraft and no party was to support a competing project. Total development costs were estimated at £190m and an in-service date was targeted for 1973.

Problems began to emerge fairly quickly. Changes in the A300 design escalated programme costs. Market support was little in evidence and political support for the project was beginning to wane. A second, and potentially more commercially attractive design, the A300B, was developed in December 1968. The British government, however, had by then decided to leave the project. Left to launch the A300B on their own, France and Germany signed a new Memorandum of Understanding allowing greater autonomy to the industrial partners and imposing strict penalties for unilateral withdrawal. Airbus Industrie was established under French law to administer and coordinate the Airbus programme. The British industrial contractor was meanwhile able to participate after negotiating a private agreement with Airbus Industrie on the basis of some financial support from the German government.

Difficulties in marketing the aircraft were exacerbated by the 1973 recession. By March 1974 only twenty aircraft had been sold. The German government viewed the escalating costs with concern, but the unwavering support of the French and the importance of Airbus to the German aircraft industry ensured that full production went ahead. In 1975 Airbus gained its first non-European orders, from

Air India and South African Airways. Sales for that year showed that within its class Airbus had achieved a substantial lead over American competitors.[15]

A permanent place in the market, however, was dependent on Airbus Industrie emulating the Boeing and MDD(US) concept of a family of airliners. By the mid-1970s, therefore, attention was focused on the A310. To cover the costs of launching a second aircraft, Airbus Industrie expanded its membership to include the Spanish firm Casa, with the Dutch company Fokker as an associate. The British government, meanwhile, was keen on promoting cooperation with Boeing, although the British airframe industry preferred a European strategy. The A310 was launched by France and Germany in February 1978. The British government, forced to decide between Boeing and Airbus, eventually announced that British Aerospace (BAe) would be allowed to join Airbus Industrie as a full partner from January 1979. By the following year Airbus had been bought by 40 airlines. A total of 292 Airbus Industrie aircraft had been sold, with 157 options.

The next Airbus design, the A320, followed market survey indications that a 150-seater along the lines of the Boeing 727 offered the best prospects for a third project in the Airbus family. France supported the idea, but Germany and Britain remained non-committal until early 1984, when the A320 had acquired a total of 88 sales and options. By December 1986 the A300 had attracted 282 sales and orders, and the A310 121, while orders for the A320 stood at 246. But these sales will not recoup the development costs invested over the years by European taxpayers.

The January 1986 decision by Airbus Industrie to launch two new projects, the A330 and A340, at a cost of around $2.5 billion raises a number of questions about the future structure and operation of the consortium. Although the two new designs will share a common development programme based on the experience of the earlier Airbus types, development costs will still require governmental support. Aerospatiale, BAe, MBB and Lufthansa want to press ahead, but the British, German and French governments are more cautious about investing in new projects so soon after the A320 launch, and are keen to promote more private investment. Airbus Industrie are actively seeking new partners to share the risk of the A330/A340 development. However, changes in the pattern of national contributions and organizational structures may well strain the successful operation of the collaboration.


### The space sector

Early activities in European collaboration in the space sector involved the emergence of two European organizational frameworks – the European Launcher Development Organization (ELDO) and the European Space Research Organization (ESRO) – in an attempt to develop a European space policy. Established in 1962, ELDO was directed towards the development of a three-stage launcher using the British Blue Streak and the French Coralie rockets. ESRO meanwhile was a non-commercial scientific organization aimed at the promotion of collaboration in space research and related technologies.

The experience of the two organizations proved somewhat different. The low level of governmental commitment to ELDO was reflected in the long delays in the ratification of its convention. By 1964 its programme timing and costs were seriously adrift. French demands for a more advanced programme in 1965 created ELDO's first major crisis, which was followed a year later by British concern over the technology's obsolescence and doubts about the wisdom of continued participation. Britain's financial contribution to ELDO was reduced and the technical programme and management modified. ESRO's experience, meanwhile, proved that European collaboration was much easier in the field of basic scientific research. Later, British preference for the purchase of off-the-shelf US technology led to a Franco-German partnership and the launching in 1970 of their combined satellite, Symphonie, using the ELDO launcher and ESRO's telemetry facilities. Although commercially non-viable, it did have the effect of unsettling the British and facilitating the development of a more coherent European space policy during the 1970s. The European Space Conference in 1973 resolved some of the intergovernmental differences, merged the two space organizations into one and agreed a new programme.

The European Space Agency (ESA) emerged and subsequently blossomed as the primary framework for civilian or 'peaceful' collaboration on space in Western Europe. Its wide membership drew in all the European countries with a keen interest in the sector, and even attracted associates from outside Europe. In all of the participating countries, governments and public agencies were the prime contractors, since so many of the early applications of space technology were used to provide public goods or as trail-blazers for subsequent commercial applications. This fact simplified the remit of ESA, which became the cornerstone of the national programmes of its members. The precise formulae used to govern work through ESA benefited from lessons learnt from ELDO and ESRO and to some extent from the experiences the aviation industry had gained in its collaboration in adjacent sectors. Interestingly, the specialized character of space technology and of ESA as the functionally oriented collaborative framework helped to produce a coherence of purpose and a close-knit community of policy-makers, scientists, engineers and industrialists. For them ESA became a highly valued forum and one which enabled the Europeans both to establish a serious, even competitive, foothold in launchers, and to develop a range of sophisticated payloads.

ESA has thus become something of a model framework for technological collaboration, both because of the way it works and because it ensured that by the mid-1980s Western Europe had the range of space capabilities that could be developed to achieve European autonomy in space. We should, however, be wary of overstating the success of ESA. Proactive French leadership of European space policy had much to do with its early achievements, especially the series of Ariane launchers. Now that there is more technological competition within Europe, fuelled partly by more assertive British and German policies, new ways will have to be found of establishing a balance among the central players. ESA's role also diminishes once collaboration moves from the more experimental to the more commercial phase of development, and this explains the separate existence of Arianespace to manage commercial launches. ESA has not, and cannot as constituted, provide a wholly effective vehicle for promoting the collective interests of the European space industry in, for example, competition against American suppliers for international contracts. Nor has ESA the instruments or legal power to determine the market conditions within Europe in, for example, telecommunications and broadcasting. The other difficulty concerns the boundary between civil and military applications of space technology, a boundary which ESA's charter and neutral members forbid it to cross, but a boundary which may well inhibit the future development of European capabilities.

## Lessons from the early European experience

The early phase of European technological collaboration produced an assorted collection of ventures and outcomes. Attempts to develop collaboration within the European Community had mixed and largely disappointing results in the 1960s and for much of the 1970s. Arguments among governments, differences of national policies and priorities and difficulties in establishing effective management formulae were all major constraints. Even so, the European Communities in general, and Euratom in particular, did play a role in fostering debate and promoting transnational contact. This was to bear fruit later in terms of specific cases such as the Debene collaboration, the diagnosis of Europe's technological needs, the emergence of such initiatives as Esprit and, eventually, a heightened awareness of the corollary policy requirements and market conditions without which European technology could not flourish.

Meanwhile, initiatives on a more restricted basis among a few partners began to emerge as a primary means of promoting European technological collaboration. The Concorde experience, although a long drawn-out saga, did succeed on a technological and organizational if not a commercial level. Perhaps only such a prestigious project would have brought the two sides together, but its very complexity made it a tall order for a first attempt at collaboration. It did act as an important ice-breaker for reluctant French and British aviation companies, and provided valuable opportunities for French systems and electronics companies. Its psychological legacy, though, should not be underestimated, not least in alerting the financiers (public and private) of large projects to the high risks of such investments and in emphasizing the need to think through the implications of collaboration.

The various aviation projects of the 1950s and 1960s point to a number of broader lessons which, though they might seem fairly obvious today, were less so at the time. Differences in language, educational training, national procedures and geography were shown not to be insuperable barriers to success. Genuinely common objectives – or, more realistically, compatible self-interests – seemed essential foundations for success. The Anglo-French VG aircraft, for example, foundered on this rock. Collaborative projects, whether civil or military, require discipline in terms of cost estimation, market assessment and control, but complex projects such as Tornado can in fact be successfuly managed at the international level. Fast breeder reactors, Airbus Industrie and civilian space via ESA all represent programmes that are currently in a mature phase of collaboration. All have involved a step-by-step progression and have demonstrated the importance of mutual trust between partners and the role played by certain key individuals in ensuring the successful continuation of a programme. Each of these cases illustrates the strength and utility of functionally specific frameworks for collaboration in sectors where go-it-alone national approaches were simply not viable.

Overall, then, the development and experience of this early phase of European collaboration reveals several major points. Technological collaboration is not easy at the best of times, even within a national context, and we must thus recognize the experimental nature of what was being attempted. Crucially, Franco-German links played a key role in several collaborative ventures, though rivalries between them were important in some instances, including many not dealt with in this chapter. The continuing tensions between French interventionism and the German commitment to the free market also inhibited the emergence of a collective European approach. We should, however, recognize that then as now this formal dichotomy of doctrine was an imperfect guide to practice, with the French often more susceptible to market judgments, and the Germans more ready to support their industrial preferences. Another striking leitmotif was the recurrent ambivalence of British governments and some companies towards European collaboration. When the British came in, they often did so late and as a junior partner in the enterprise. Finally, an unresolved issue throughout was the relationship between the USA and Europe in terms of the extent of US penetration of the European market, the question of how to access US technology without conceding dependency and the problem of whether European initiatives should include American partners.

As Chapter 1 points out, however, any lessons from the collaborative experience really need to be defined in relation to whether the particular formulae adopted served the appropriate economic, industrial and public policy needs. One criterion is the rate of commercial return on the finances invested, whether public or private. Viewed from this perspective only Airbus Industrie might be considered a commercial success, but even this must be qualified. Much hinges on the fortunes of the A320, which has the chance of being profitable as a venture, though not all of the development costs of the earlier aircraft will be recouperable. For fast breeder reactors, meanwhile, commercialization has become a receding target. Another *raison d'être* of European collaboration has been the concern to ensure the long-term survival of an industrial sector, always an important part of the aviation story and increasingly relevant, in the 1980s, to fast breeder reactors. Beyond this, at least in the aviation and space examples, lies the tantalizing question of what would otherwise have been the case. European governments could have 'saved' direct expenditure on Airbus only to be forced to pay, albeit more indirectly, higher prices for American aeroplanes. The Ariane space launcher has been expensive to produce, but US shuttle launches might otherwise have been more expensive and in any case are not currently a viable alternative.

Clearly, demonstrable learning curves constitute a second type of return on collaboration. In the Airbus programme, for example, the A300 was the first step in a collaborative learning curve. The A300 established Airbus Industrie as the centre for large-scale civil aircraft production in Europe, and the A320 confirmed that Airbus Industrie was a force to be reckoned with in European aerospace policy.[16] Similarly, a learning curve is discernible in fast breeder reactor collaboration, although its basis is technological and managerial rather than commercial. The 1984 Memorandum builds on previous experience to develop the concept of a 'European' reactor model applicable across the board. And, of course, the mixed records of ELDO and ESRO were critical in determining a pattern within ESA which was more effective.

The experience of the 1960s and early 1970s shows that a variety of collaborative modes are available. It does not necessarily matter whether the arrangements are bilateral, trilateral or multilateral so long as they operate economically and efficiently. It is crucial that the partners involved perceive sufficient benefits in the longer term to sustain their commitment and to find ways of reconciling major differences in outlook and interests. Similarly, the interweaving of governmental and industrial roles is significant. As one commentator on Airbus has recently remarked, its achievements were 'largely the result of bilateral or trilateral contacts and negotiations between both officials and industrialists. Both were indispensable.'[17] In fast breeder reactors, too, intergovernmental agreements and negotiations provided crucial support in the Debene and, later, the Franco-Italian and Serena partnerships.[18] Most important, perhaps, is the need to build in scope for review and reappraisal, even withdrawal. Without this, collaborative ventures run the risk of encouraging expensive white elephants or discouraging adaptation and innovation.

# 3

# COMMUNITY INITIATIVES IN THE 1980s

In contrast to the two preceding decades, the 1980s have been marked by a striking faith in the ability of industrial collaboration to cure Europe's relative lack of competitiveness and by a consequent rash of government-backed initiatives to stimulate joint R&D between European companies. A number of schemes have been sponsored within the European Communities, the most important of which has been Esprit (European Strategic Programme for Research and Development in Information Technology). Designed as a strategic programme to improve Europe's technological base, Esprit encourages collaboration between companies, universities and research institutes on a wide range of areas in information technology. Its sister programme in the telecommunications sphere, Race (R&D in Advanced Communications Technologies for Europe), is intended to lay the groundwork for a new generation of optical fibre broadband communications systems expected to come into service in Europe during the 1990s. These and other important Community initiatives are the subject of this chapter (see Table 3.1). Outside the European Community, a number of industry-to-industry private initiatives have emerged, together with the Eureka initiative, which was launched by the French government in 1985 and attracted support from nineteen European governments before emerging as a loosely knit framework. These activities will be examined in Chapter 4.

Why should this spate of initiatives occur at this specific moment? Part of the answer lies in the reincarnation of the notion of Europe's technology gap. However, as Chapter 1 points out, much of the surrounding rhetoric masks a quite fundamental switch in the argument. Prior to the 1980s the underlying assumption was that market size was required mainly to secure the necessary economies of scale in production. Only in computers was the issue of R&D a dominant one. By the early 1980s, however, R&D had become a prime concern of many European industries, faced as they were with the globalization of competition, US predominance and Japanese success. The logic behind this new industrial collaboration was therefore based on the need to spread both costs and the market-entry risks for new products at a time when technologies were converging, the pace of technological development was accelerating and development costs were rising.

A second factor was the French commitment to the idea of European collaboration, especially in information technology and telecommunications. France had been foremost among European governments in campaigning for a united European front in the struggle to gain a larger share in the global electronics and information processing markets, and it had called for the creation of strategic telecommunications alliances, the liberalization of procurement policies and harmonization of standards. Such exhortations began to have an impact at the intergovernmental, if not at the industrial, level. The mid-1970s, for example, saw the emergence of a new Franco-German willingness to collaborate in the field of microelectronics. In a series of meetings held during 1976–7, agreement was reached on the need for a European microelectronics programme. Discussions with the European Commission and key industrial managers resulted in the establishment of a technical group whose aim was to define the objectives of what would have been a European VLSI programme to match the Japanese equivalent. In the event, the understanding fell apart. Cautious about sharing their know-how on new product developments with weaker partners, the largest companies (including Philips and Siemens) displayed a marked preference for the acquisition of American technology. The French and German governments in the

Table 3.1 Sample of major European Community programmes

| Programme | Date | Duration | Budget | Emphasis | Future plans |
|---|---|---|---|---|---|
| Bep | 1982 | 4 years | 15 mecus | Promotion of academic/industrial links; support of post-doctoral training and exchange | Succeeded by Bap |
| Esprit | 1983 (Pilot phase) | 1 year | 11.5 mecus | Microelectronics, software technology, advanced information processing, office systems, computer integrated manufacture | Phase 2 (5 years) |
| | 1984 (Phase 1) | 5 years | 750 mecus | | |
| Race | 1985 (Definition phase) | 18 months | 40 mecus | Establishment of a technological base for the introduction of a Community-wide IBCN telecommunications infrastructure and services | Phase 2 (5 years) |
| | 1987 (Phase 1) | 5 years | currently being decided | | |
| Brite | 1985 | 4 years | 125 mecus | Development of advanced technologies to support traditional industries within the EC | |
| Bap | 1986 | 5 years | 50 mecus | Promotion of research and training and contextual developments in enzyme, genetic and protein engineering | |
| Comett | 1986 | 4 years | 80 mecus | European network of university/industry training partnerships | Phase 2 (3 years) |

Compiled by Claire Shearman, February 1987.

meantime, while displaying a real desire and will to collaborate, were never fully on the same wavelength as to how to do so.[1] The French government also linked the notion of European technological collaboration to wider policy issues. Its attempt in autumn 1982 to link high-technology activities with policy on both intra- and extra-Community trade was not well received by the British and Germans. Undeterred, however, it continued to pursue the notion of a European collaboration strategy with a proposal, in its September 1983 Memorandum, for 'un espace industriel européen' (i.e. industrial *area*), with a call for a European Space Community in February 1984, and with recommendations for greater efforts within the EC in the areas of industrial, technological and social policy.

Outside the government Jacques Delors, then an MEP, had come up with the idea of 'géometrie variable'. This advocated selective European collaboration in particular policy areas, and especially industrial sectors, to complement the core areas dealt with by the European Community. Thus, as Helen Wallace has commented, the French were developing ideas which were later to emerge not only in the Commission's proposals for a European Technology Community, but also in the rationale underlying both the 'espace industriel européen' and the Eureka programme (see Chapter 4).[2]

A further important factor behind the recent spate of collaboration initiatives is the way in which many European industrialists have begun to think collectively in terms of a European dimension to their activities, much as their scientific counterparts did in the 1960s. This change of attitude was facilitated by the European Commission, whose efforts over the past decade to involve industrialists in Community policies have had the side effect of providing a European forum for discussions and contacts. In the context of the current economic climate, the result has been the emergence of what might be described as a 'European' industrial consciousness. This in itself provides a potent force for collaboration and, if productive, may well be self-generating.

The following selective review of the more important initiatives within the Community serves to identify those factors which have contributed to their apparent success. Most of the programmes are the fruits of ideas developed over a considerable length of time.

Esprit, Race and Brite all involved a lengthy process of consultation and consensus-building. Their emergence coincided with other crucial developments, notably the perceived threat to Europe from Japanese as well as American industry and the effects of a prolonged recession. A number of people – not just the high-profile instigators such as Vicomte Davignon, but also many officials at the operating level – played a central role in developing and steering the various proposals through the policy-making process.

**The European Community: building for the 1980s**
During the 1960s and 1970s the sectors caught up in European collaboration – aviation, nuclear energy and space – were considered to be of strategic importance. The computing sector, by contrast, was not subject to governmental dominance; nor did it receive sustained attention as a strategic industry. Collaborative activities at the European level were slow to get off the ground. Several attempts were made during the 1960s to develop cross-national groupings but most turned out to be somewhat inconclusive. In 1962, for example, talks between Siemens, Olivetti, ICL and Bull failed to reach any agreement. In 1969 the Eurodata consortium – comprising ICL, CII, Philips, AEG-Telefunken, Saab and Olivetti – was established to tender for an ESRO computer requirement, but in the event pressure from Siemens on the German government against this move led to the collapse of the deal.

During the mid-1960s the British, French and German governments sought to develop their national champions. It was against this backcloth that the Unidata experiment was enacted. Arising out of a Franco-German bilateral link, Unidata seemed to offer a means of creating a European IBM. Governments were to combine their national programmes in support of the group, whose aim was jointly to develop and market a new range of computers. The industrialists involved suggested that thorough collaboration required a merger under a single management, but this solution was unacceptable to the French government, which wanted Honeywell-Bull and CII to merge under 51 per cent French ownership and be party to a global arrangement to market and share products with Honeywell US. This deal was intended to combine French control with access to advanced technology. French failure to consult either the German government or Siemens embittered relations and contributed to Unidata's subsequent collapse. The episode also revealed the difficulty of embarking on collaboration at so late a stage in the product cycle. It was not until the late 1970s that the strategic significance of computing and information technology was widely recognized on a European scale.

A Council Resolution on data processing had been adopted by the EEC in 1974, when expectations for the success of Unidata were high. Unidata's subsequent collapse undermined the Commission's activities, with the result that a medium-term programme on the application, development and production of data-processing systems failed to be implemented. Instead the Commission pursued a series of isolated activities and supported little R&D that was industrially significant.

But by the end of the decade the climate had altered. Changes in governments, rising unemployment and the disappointments of nationally based approaches led policy-makers in Europe to rethink the Community's role in industrial R&D. The Commission, which had long recognized the problem, changed its approach, and the resulting priorities for research were set out in a new form called the Framework Programme. In 1979 Vicomte Davignon took over the Commission's industry portfolio. His interest in industrial R&D became evident at the same time as DG XII's forward-looking Europe +30 exercise reached fruition and the Fast (Forecasting and Assessment in Science and Technology) group studies on the information society, biotechnology, and work and employment were endorsed as useful. These indicated Europe's weakness in translating basic research into industrial activities and proved instrumental in influencing the move of DG XII's Director-General Günter Schuster towards a more industrially oriented R&D policy.

Under Davignon's guidance the Commission began to develop a more strategic approach to the information technology sector. A programme on microelectronic technology was produced in 1979–80 and agreed by the Council in November 1981. The Commission then took the unorthodox step of inviting representatives from the major companies to establish a working group and to draw up a programme. Although delays in the Community's decision-making process postponed the programme's launch for almost a year, 30 mecus (million European currency units) were eventually allocated as a 'European' response to a similar but larger-scale initiative in the USA.[3]

## The development of the Esprit programme

*Setting the context: national responses to Europe's weakness*

In the early 1980s many industrialists began to express concern at Europe's relative decline in the IT sector. Within the industry as a whole, the European Community supplied a mere 40 per cent of its own market and 10 per cent of the world market. Whereas in 1975 the EC balance of payments in IT goods and services had been positive, by 1982 a large deficit had arisen. Japan meanwhile seemed intent on becoming the IT industry's second world leader. Its Fifth Generation computer programme, involving some $200m-$500m of government financial investment, was launched in October 1981. The USA, too, was far from complacent. Department of Defense collaborative programmes included work on VLSI, the STARS programme in software engineering and the Strategic Computing programme to develop supercomputers performing high-speed scientific calculations. Privately sponsored ventures included the Computer Aided Manufacturing International and the Semiconductor Research Cooperative established by the major US manufacturers.

Various initiatives by individual European governments sought to respond to these moves, building on their disparate efforts in the 1970s. France initiated the Plan d'Action Filière Electronique in 1982 and established a programme of microelectronics support; Germany established research programmes in microelectronics, CAD/CAM, optoelectronics and telecommunications; and Britain responded with the Alvey programme. This last emerged from the deliberations of a committee headed by John Alvey, Senior Director of Technology at British Telecom. Established in March 1982, the committee concluded that pre-competitive collaborative research between industry and universities was an essential component in matching technical expertise with commercial objectives, and it identified four key enabling technologies: software engineering, man-machine interfaces, intelligent knowledge-based systems (IKBS) and very large-scale integration of circuits on silicon. Although the Alvey committee recommended 100 per cent funding, the British government finally agreed on a five-year programme costing £350m, only £200m of which was to be government-financed.

*Davignon and the Round Table*
Commissioner Davignon played a vital role in developing the Esprit programme. In his evidence to a recent House of Lords Select Committee on the European Communities, he outlined the three factors which had motivated his attempts.[4] In the first place, he had been struck by the 'very distinctive difference of performance' between the USA, Japan and the EC. Second, he had felt that the time had come for Community competences to be adjusted so as to reflect more accurately the state-of-the-art; and, third, he had been aware of the fact that no real incentive existed for cross-border collaboration. Any Community-level solution therefore needed a new approach to policy development. Davignon determined to liaise with only the very highest levels of company management and to define any priority areas for action with, rather than for, them.

Over the period 1979–80 Davignon therefore invited the heads of Europe's leading electronics and IT companies to a series of Round Table discussions. The 'Big Twelve', as they came to be known, comprised ICL, GEC and Plessey from Britain; AEG, Nixdorf and Siemens from Germany; Thomson, Bull and CGE from France; Olivetti and STET from Italy; and Philips from the Netherlands. Davignon's objective was to initiate debate on how the technology gap which had opened between Europe and the USA and Japan might best be closed. Thus the original ideas underlying Esprit predated the launch of Japan's Fifth Generation programme and involved a much wider remit, namely, to meet the challenge across the board in IT, computing and telecommunications.

Having brought Europe's top-level IT managers together, Davignon received a more favorable response than when their lower-level counterparts had met with the Commission two years earlier. A technical committee was established which later became the steering committee. This in turn set up a number of technical panels and workshops. Discussions continued for a couple of years. Initially attention was focused on the way in which a European collaborative response could be promoted at the business level, that is, on how to encourage joint companies which would not otherwise have been established to manufacture products within Europe. Such activities, however, proved difficult to organize from the top down, whereas the concept of carrying out a major collaborative research programme seemed a more appropriate activity on a Community basis.[5] Discussion therefore focused on the pre-competitive end of collaborative research, a stance which from the Commission's viewpoint neatly avoided the issue of competition policy.

The emergence of a Round Table consensus on the five areas of research where a European programme was deemed essential quite clearly reflected a high level of industrial commitment. Discussions had been lengthy and involved at a time when the possibility of any form of Community programme or funding was uncertain. Yet industry's willingness to commit itself was the result both of the intensified competition in information technology globally and of the behind-the-scenes influence of the Gyllenhammer group. This European round table of industrialists (not to be confused with the Esprit Round Table) represents an informal grouping of European manufacturers, ranging from Philips to Volvo to Pilkingtons, who keep a watching brief on infrastructural issues affecting Europe in general. Their acknowledgment of the inefficacy of promoting solely national policies played a role in the realization of Esprit, as did the careful work of certain DG XII officials and the newly formed alliance between the Commission and industry, which brought pressure to bear on national governments.

*The early stages*
These various strands were important in getting Esprit off the ground. An outline proposal was produced in September 1980. In May 1982 the Council received the Commission's official Esprit document, 'Towards a European Strategic Programme for Research and Development in Information Technology'.[6] This pointed to the need for a European strategic programme to provide the basic technology necessary to compete with Japan and the USA. Five priority areas of pre-competitive research were identified (see below) in which the major European companies and their smaller counterparts, universities and research institutes would be brought together.

The Commission's proposals received a favourable response at both the June Council meeting and the Versailles European Council of June 1982. Encouraged, the Commission put forward detailed proposals in August 1982 for a pilot scheme which the Council agreed to the following December with an allocation of 11.5 mecus.

The remaining 50 per cent of the costs were to be provided by industry.

### The pilot phase

The Commission called for proposals for the Esprit pilot phase in February 1983. The idea was to gain some pre-launch experience in order to provide the basis for a better management scheme for the overall programme. Of the 200 submissions received by the Commission, only about one-third were of the right technical quality or met the Esprit criteria for transnational partnership. Projects were selected that spring by six independent panels appointed by the Commission. Contracts began to be signed during May, and from September 1983 onwards 38 projects were launched which were later to be incorporated into the main part of the programme. Over 80 per cent of the first round of contracts went to the twelve Round Table companies (but then they comprised 70 per cent of the industry). The majority involved participants from two to three member states. Of the total number of organizations associated with the pilot phase, 27 were located in Britain, 21 in Germany, 10 in the Netherlands, 8 in Belgium, 4 in France and 2 in Italy. Examples of the projects are the Thomson-CSF partnership with Plessey and GEC in the development of an advanced interconnect for VLSI with Telefunken Elektronik and the Universities of Newcastle, Southampton and Montpellier; the collaboration between Siemens, System Designers Ltd, CIT Alcatel and Philips on software production and maintenance management systems; and that between Olivetti and Nixdorf in broadbased office communication systems.[7]

### The full Esprit programme

Once the full pilot phase was under way, the Commission sent the Council a proposal for a ten-year Esprit programme (1984–93) with a 1,500 mecus budget in total. The first five-year phase would represent some 10,000 person years of research concentrating on generic information technologies (microelectronics, advanced information processing and software technology) and two fields of applications (office systems and computer integrated manufacturing).

The Commission's proposals were generally well received. The workplan had been drawn up by six specialist panels and, together with proposals on telecommunications and biotechnology, was put to the Council in November 1983. British and German reservations over the budgetary costs delayed the final approval of Esprit until February 1984.

A first call for proposals for the main Esprit programme was issued the following month, and met with a huge response of 441 serious submissions. These were evaluated by 60 experts during May and June, and a shortlist was drawn up in July. The 201 projects eventually selected for the programme's first phase involved 240 firms (57 per cent of these with less than 500 employees) and 210 research institutions. Three-quarters of the research projects involve collaboration between firms and academic research units. As of January 1987, the total cost was 1.36 billion ecus.

*Programme content and objectives*
Esprit's fundamental objective is to create a competitive European industry in information technology. Specifically it aims to provide the necessary technological base and to encourage cross-border pre-competitive industrial R&D collaboration. The intention is also to create a substantial spin-off, not only in terms of future collaboration at the product development or manufacturing stage, but also as a momentum towards the progressive establishment of common European IT standards. For these, collaboration at the early stages is often crucial.

As noted above, Esprit focuses on five areas of R&D activity. These are advanced microelectronic capability, software technology, advanced information processing, office systems and computer-integrated manufacture. In the advanced microelectronic sector, the aim is to provide the technical ability to design, manufacture and test very high-speed and very large-scale integrated circuits. Esprit's approach to software technology focuses on formal mathematical techniques, the software production process and development of software as a product. Projects in advanced information processing are designed to create a basis for the industrial exploitation of the transition from data processing and computation to knowledge processing. Activities under investigation in the office systems section include office work-stations and communication systems, office filing and retrieval systems, man-machine interaction and machine translation. Finally, the computer-integrated manufacture section aims to establish the technology base required for the application of information technology to the manufacturing cycle and the ultimate development of fully integrated manufacturing systems.

Crucial features include the conditions of participation. Project proposals have to be submitted in reply to open invitations. Each project must involve at least two independent industrial partners from separate member states. Costs are generally co-financed by the Community and industry on a 50/50 basis. Research results are shared between all the participants in any given project who are free to apply them commercially, and preferential access is then granted to other Esprit participants outside that project. These guarantees are cornerstones of the whole Esprit process.

The programme was defined and managed from the Commission by a specially created Task Force for Information Technology and Telecommunications, many of whose personnel were drawn from industry and the academic world. The Task Force was an important management tool, and has been absorbed since January 1987 in DG XIII. The Esprit Advisory Board draws on expert opinion from both producers and users, while the final say on project selection rests with the member states' representatives on the Esprit Management Committee.

### *The Esprit review procedure*
The Council decision adopting the Esprit programme required the Commission to review its progress after 30 months or as soon as 60 per cent of the first-phase budget had been committed. A three-person Review Board conducted interviews and surveys to assess: the extent to which Esprit was achieving its original objectives; the programme's administration; its relationship with national programmes; information dissemination; and the communication flows among participants. The Board's report of October 1985 concluded that Esprit had been successfully established and was well on its way to meeting its original objectives. Certain changes in the selection procedure and evaluation of proposals were suggested, together with improvements in project management and additional channels of communication. For the future development of Esprit the Board pointed to a continued emphasis on the pre-competitive aspect of research, a consolidation and restructuring of research areas and, finally, the addition of focused demonstration projects with a large user-involvement. Three areas of research were suggested for this: microelectronics, advanced information processing (incorporating

the current software technology) and applications (merging the current categories of office systems and computer-integrated manufacture). Optoelectronics, although falling under the Race remit, might also require additional support under Esprit.[8]

These suggestions were incorporated in the second phase of the programme, which the Commision hopes will start in 1987. The aim is a programme roughly three times the size of Esprit I (30,000 instead of 10,000 research hours) with a budget of 2 billion ecus. The Review Board's recommendations were accepted, and the three main areas of research are microelectronics, IT processing systems and applications technologies. It is proposed that the programme will be 'demand driven': for example, in microelectronics, projects will focus on technologies relevant to the development of ASIC chips, a growing market in which Europe is seen to have some advantages. The idea of demonstration projects is carried over to what are called 'Technology Integration Projects' (TIPs), the aim of which is to pull the various strands of work together to show their usefulness to one another. For example, work on desk-top work-stations is being linked to the more theoretical work on parallel architectures, and, if successful, this combination will considerably enhance the processing and presentation capabilities of the work-stations.

The evaluation process continues and is now beginning to generate appraisals of the results of Esprit projects, for example in the report entitled 'Esprit, the First Phase: Progress and Results' (COM (86) 687, 8 December 1986).

### Esprit's effect on standards

One of the most important spin-offs from the Esprit programme has been in the field of European IT standards. Here the debate has centred on the relative merits of adopting the Open Systems Interconnection (OSI) model being evolved by the International Standards Organization (ISO) or adhering to the Systems Network Architecture approach deployed as a *de facto* standard by IBM. The former provides for the interworking of systems with different architectures, while the latter opts for a complete network service within a coherent architectural framework.

The Commission has long been active in the standards field, but more intensively since the early 1980s. Current Community policy recognizes ISO and CCITT standards and recommendations, and the Commission both coordinates with and puts pressure on the European agencies for technical standardization, CEPT and CEN/CENELEC. Priority areas for development are standards for open communication networks; high levels of OSI standards; message-handling, teletext and document exchange; formal description techniques and programming languages. Additional priorities for the telecommunications sector include ISDN, mobile cellular telephony, telematic terminals and broadband networks. Two Working Groups, one on Standards and the other on Standardization Aspects of Public Procurement, have been established under the Multiannual Data Processing Programme; activities have been coordinated within the European Workshop on Informatics and Computing Systems; and a computer hardware procurement policy based on the work of the Standards Implementation Committee has been developed. Directive 83/189/EEC enabled member states to exchange information on planned draft standards, and the European Commission to conclude agreements with the relevant bodies. One achievement here has been the agreement on the mutual recognition of type approvals for telecommunications terminal equipment. More recently, the Commission has been involved in the setting up of European IT and telecommunications conformity testing services. To date 15 centres have agreed to develop the necessary facilities and procedures.

Esprit industrialists have provided considerable support for the Commission's activities. For example, it was their decision in early 1984 to adopt common interconnection standards. In addition, their suggestion for a prospective rather than retrospective European Information Technology Standards Policy at Community level provided the Commission with much of its impetus. Participation in Esprit has moreover motivated some industrialists to generate their own activities in standards. Work in OSI has received a major boost with the creation in March 1983 of the Standards Promotion and Application Group (SPAG). This consortium of the twelve leading European computer firms is seeking common communications protocols to help customers build their information systems with products from different vendors. Its recent results have been followed by the establishment of the Corporation for Open Systems (COS) and an Open Systems Promotion Conference in Japan. In June 1986 ICL took a European Companies' Initiative with its major European analogues to push ahead for OSI and the other requirements for opening the European market.

In addition, eight of the SPAG members have agreed to establish common testing facilities through a new company, Spag Services, which will validate compatible operating standards for a wide range of data processing and office automation equipment. This is an important step in the development of the European computer and information technology industry, since companies to date have been hampered by the use of a variety of functional standards governing the way pieces of equipment communicate. By adopting a common standard, European groups will now be able to offer their customers equipment that is compatible with products from other European manufacturers and thus generate more non-IBM competition. Even so, progress towards the development of IT standards within Europe has been slow, because of the vested interests at national level, the differing approaches of the various authorities, the inherent technical complexities of the task and the sometimes cumbersome functioning of international bodies.

## Community initiatives in telecommunications
*The European context*
The 1980s have seen a number of changes in telecommunications in Europe. Since Britain liberalized its market in 1981, France, Germany and the Netherlands have all launched reviews of their national policies. The overcrowded telecommunications equipment industry has led to a certain amount of rationalization, most evidently in France, where CGE agreed a joint venture with ITT from the USA to create the world's second largest manufacturer with operations across a number of countries. Although other interests in the CGE 'European' consortium have so far been confined to the Société Générale de Belgique – with the failure to secure German support and Spanish satisfaction – the deal nevertheless represents the most ambitious attempt to date to form a new manufacturing alliance capable of attacking global markets. CGE also awaits a French governmental decision on its proposed alliance with AT&T/Philips, while AT&T, Siemens, Ericsson and Northern Telecom (Canada) are currently competing for ownership of the rival and soon to be privatized CGCT.

The European telecommunications industry is currently facing a number of pressures. Technological convergence is eroding traditional boundaries, not only between computing and telecommunications but also in relation to other industries such as financial services, retailing, cable TV and satellite services. International competition has been fuelled by US deregulation and the break-up of American Telephone and Telegraph (AT&T). Large business consumers are demanding a wider service choice and lower tariffs while development costs are soaring. Despite these common problems, Europe has witnessed a diversity of response. Different countries are moving at different speeds towards different goals, presenting the Commission with a major problem in its efforts to secure the development of a Europe-wide telecommunications infrastructure.

*The Race programme*
The development of the Race programme has proved quite a slow and difficult task for the European Commission. Unlike Esprit, Race requires for its successful implementation the consent of national PTTs as customers and the reconciliation of major differences in national interests and approaches. The Esprit model was therefore not appropriate and the Commission had instead to engage the interests of the relevant parties more indirectly via member governments (though having paved the way with Esprit helped). Race thus reflects a new consensus that the currently evolving narrowband Integrated Services Digital Network (ISDN) should gradually be replaced by an Integrated Broadband Communications Network (IBCN).[9] Race is designed to establish the technological base essential to the introduction of a Community-wide IBCN infrastructure and services. The programme's definition phase (1985–6) is aimed at agreeing an IBCN reference model, identifying the relevant R&D and design work, developing a consensus among PTTs on the functional and technoeconomic characteristics of the network itself, and evaluating the technical environment and the applications and/or services made possible by the new network.[10]

In February 1986 the formal go-ahead was given for the Race definition phase, following earlier initiatives by the Commission. From September 1985 onwards, 171 organizations responded to the call for proposals with 80 project suggestions covering the whole range of telecommunications. Leading experts selected 32 proposals involving 109 organizations, and these in turn were converted into projects which together form a coherent programme. Those involved in this IBCN definition phase include the telecommunications administrations, broadcasters, university researchers and manufacturers such as Plessey, STC and Thorn EMI (UK), CIT Alcatel (France), Siemens (Germany) and Italtel (Italy). Broadly speaking the R&D falls into the areas of integrated circuits, optoelectronics, broadband switching and communications software. Work began on some projects in early 1986. Since then all the contracts have been negotiated. Total costs, to be shared between the Commission and the participants, are in the range of 40 mecus.

The Race definition phase runs for 18 months. The results will fall into two categories: the specification of the Integrated Advanced Network as designated by the telecommunications administration, and the design work by the manufacturers of the terminal equipment required to deliver advanced services for business and private consumers. Already this work has served to reduce dramatically the number of scenarios for new schemes under investigation. Two further stages in the programme are envisaged. The object of the first phase (1987–92) will be to develop the technological base for IBCN, formulate common proposals for specifications and standards, and carry out the necessary pre-competitive developments for IBCN demonstration equipment. The Commission submitted proposals for this round of the programme in October 1986, with a budget of 800 mecus. The Council approved the plans, but final agreement depended on settlement of the budget for the Framework Programme. Phase 2 (1992–7) will then aim to develop the technological base for enhanced IBCN equipment and services.

Race has been supported by a number of other Community initiatives. Some of the R&D work, for example, overlaps with the Esprit programme. More specifically, the Commission has adopted a draft recommendation to coordinate the introduction of ISDN into the Community. Member states have been asked to recommend to their PTT administrations a series of innovations based on the combined use of digital telephones and computers. The Commission sees this as one way of upgrading existing telecommunications networks, although it will take till 1993 to acquire a mature ISDN system. As in Esprit, common standards are vital. Ministers of industry have sanctioned the establishment of common standards for the new generation of telecommunications systems, and in November 1986 they agreed on a fourteen-month timetable for the definition of eleven services – including improved teletext, telephones able to take messages while the subscriber is on the phone and calling-line identification – by the end of 1987. The plan avoids over-complicated debates between member states on technical standards by producing the general framework and leaving it to national telecommunications authorities to sort out the details.

On a broader level, and in an attempt to redress the infrastructural inequalities that currently exist within Europe's telecommunications systems, the Commission has proposed the Star programme to improve the access of less-favoured Community regions and countries to advanced telecommunications services. A multiannual allocation of 750 mecus from the European Regional Development Fund would provide for both the installation of modern telecommunications equipment and a series of aid measures to boost the supply and demand for such services.[11]

### The COST framework

Some telecommunications R&D is being carried out within the COST framework. Chapter 2 describes how this was established in 1971 as a framework for the preparation and implementation of European projects involving applied scientific research. Since then its coverage has expanded. COST's open-ended approach to collaboration gives it a greater degree of flexibility and freedom than is normally the case in Community initiatives, and allows it to extend its remit beyond the confines of EC membership. Most of the projects have centred on pre-competitive research, but in a few cases COST collaboration has led directly to the development of new products, such as the so-called COST 211 codex. Used extensively for videoconference applications, this has been adopted as a European CEPT telecommunications standard and is manufactured in France, Germany and Britain.

Telecommunications has been the largest of the COST research areas (see Chapter 2), with 18 projects having been undertaken to date. Six are directly relevant to Race. Close links are also maintained with CEPT, the organization which links European post and telecommunications administrations. The main research areas covered by COST are telecommunications networks, system studies (such as optical fibres and land-mobile radiocommunications), technology developments (new antennae and high-definition television coding) and information services (man-made communications). A further eight projects are in the pipeline, dealing with such areas as human factors in information services and future telecommunications and teleinformatics facilities for disabled people.[12]

## The collaboration bandwagon

### The Brite programme
Apart from work in the IT and telecommunications sectors, the Commission's most recent major collaboration initiative has been the Brite (Basic Research in Industrial Technologies for Europe) programme. Inspired by Esprit and launched in early 1985, it aims to stimulate the development of advanced technologies to support traditional industries within the Community such as chemicals and textiles. Nine major technological 'themes' have been identified. These are the problems of reliability, wear and deterioration of materials and systems; laser technology and power metallurgy; joining techniques; new testing methods; computer-aided design and manufacturing; polymers, composites and other new materials; membrane science and technology; catalysis and particle technology; and new technologies applied to articles made from flexible materials.[13]

Brite follows the Esprit model in terms of its organization and the emphasis on pre-competitive research. The rules and procedures for project selection, partner criteria and property rights are similar. So too are the funding arrangements. The first phase (1985–8) has a projected budget of 125 mecus, and the programme to date involves over 400 organizations across the Community. Of these, 24 per cent are what the Commission describes as small and medium-sized firms, 21 per cent research institutes and 19 per cent universities. Examples of projects include the collaboration between two British and two German companies on the development of high-temperature resistant (250°-350°C) polyamide composites; the involvement of five laboratories (two German and one Belgian, French and British) in a study of flexible products based on synthetic fibres and material for industrial or agricultural use; and the cooperation between three British firms and one German in the clothing sector on the development of a fully automated assembly and sewing process.

## Community programmes in biotechnology

Biotechnology, the industrial use of biological organisms and their derivatives, is an area of rapidly expanding activity that has been fuelled by major scientific breakthroughs in molecular genetics. Its impact is wide: from the pharmaceutical industry, to chemicals, energy, waste management and, above all, agriculture and the agro-food sector.

At a European level, the first collaboration came with the establishment of the European Molecular Biology Laboratory at Heidelberg in 1978 as a multinational research centre among the European nations. Financed by direct subscription from national governments, it has now trained several generations of research scientists. Within the EC, biotechnology was one of the first areas seen by the newly constituted DG XII (Research and Technology) as ripe for collaboration. Proposals aimed at advancing strengths in genetic engineering and enzymology were first put forward in 1974, but it was not until 1981 that the Commission was given the go-ahead to introduce its Biomolecular Engineering Programme (Bep). This ran for four years (1982–5) with total expenditures of only 15 mecus, and it concentrated on supporting programmes that promoted post-doctoral training and exchange, and projects that linked academic research and industry.

Bep was succeeded in 1986 by the more ambitious Biotechnology Action Programme (Bap), which has a budget of 50 mecus for five years (1986–90). Emphasis still rests on enzyme, genetic and protein engineering, but the programme now has two main thrusts: first, as before, to promote basic research and training; and, second, to promote what are termed 'contextual' developments, specifically 'biotic' collections (i.e., cell and gene banks) and 'bio-informatics' (data banks of gene sequences, etc.).

As a result of the credibility that the Bep established for itself, the Bap initiatives have been considerably oversubscribed. In the first round of applications in early 1986, over 800 were received, 40 per cent of which involved industrial association. Given the money available only 120 (15 per cent) could be funded. In a link-up with the Esprit programme and DG XIII, the bio-informatics programme has established the Biceps (Bio-informatics Collaborative European Programme) initiative with the aim of linking and extending data availability among participants, and developing modelling techniques based on this data.

In addition to the Bap, there is the Concertation Unit for Biotechnology in Europe (Cube), which really grew out of the Fast Programme, which had identified the Bio-Society as a vital area of future development and had recognized the need for some coordination at a European level. Cube's main functions are to help the EC (both Commission and member governments) 'get its act together'. In this capacity it is linked both to the Bap and, via the Biotechnology steering group, to a range of activities such as raw material supply, agriculture, intellectual property rights and patents. In all of these areas, biotechnology challenges established practice. If Europe is to make the most of its intellectual resources in this area (and they are substantial), there is an obvious need to develop a common regulatory framework in place of the heterogeneous national regulations that currently exist. Similarly, the Convention on the European Patent should be urgently accepted by all member states (although Europe has already put itself at a disadvantage by not copying the US practice of offering a six-month period of grace between publication and patenting).

Perhaps the most urgent action required is that on the interface between agriculture and biotechnology. Protective measures for sugar crippled early developments in high fructose syrup (a sweetener obtained from starch feedstocks), which in turn effectively put paid to promising enzyme (glucose isomerase) developments in Europe (in the process giving competitive advantage to the USA and Japan). Likewise, the high-price regime for cereals and starch products caused much starch-based fermentation activity (e.g., the production of antibiotics) to shift from Community to non-Community countries, such as Austria. The recent introduction of a dual-price regime with cheap prices for cereals and starch products used as industrial raw materials has alleviated this distortion, but it still has to be seen whether the Community can effectively police such a regime. However, since biotechnology is likely, over time, to replace a number of field-based products with factory production methods, the problems over sugar and cereals are probably only the first of many such episodes.

*Cross-sectoral initiatives*
As well as these sectoral initiatives, the Community has begun to develop a range of measures to promote more extensive collaboration. Two initiatives of note are Comett (Community in Education and Training for Technology) and Rare (Associated Networks for European Research).[14] The former is designed to foster cooperation between universities and industry in training for new technologies. Rare by contrast is an association of networks and their users acting independently of manufacturers and governments and aiming to establish a communications infrastructure within Europe. Over the longer term these various activities may have an important contribution to make to changes in the research and industrial cultures and approaches within Western Europe.

## The fruits of collaboration

*Emerging trends*
While it is still too early for any full evaluation of these initiatives, experience to date points to a number of trends. First, the European Community is providing a more amenable forum for industrial collaboration than hitherto. The Commission's move away from its earlier focus on an all-embracing type of 'European' science and technology policy to the 'framework programme' approach of recent years has enabled it to develop a more flexible and task-oriented element in its organizational structure. This, together with the benefits accrued from the Esprit experience, is being transferred to similar initiatives in other policy areas within the Framework Programme. Built into this more flexible approach to technology policy-making is a recognition by the Commission of the need to promote a careful process of consensus-building. In addition to securing more effective policy implementation, this has resulted in certain alliances between industrialists and the European Commission which have served, in the cases of Esprit and Brite in particular, to facilitate the acceptance of Community programmes.[15]

Second, and especially in the case of Esprit, the effects of what might be termed a collaboration 'community' are in evidence.

63

Formal and informal channels of communication have been established between the various participants from industry, universities and research centres. A momentum has been achieved through the actual process of collaboration, the spin-off and diffusion effects of which may prove more important than the programmes themselves in terms of the contacts generated, the experience gained and the increasing acceptance of common standards. The extent of such a 'community', however, should not be exaggerated. Although it is certainly quite marked by comparison with former levels, many companies in Western Europe still have little knowledge of each other and consequently fail to exploit much of the potential that Europe might offer them.

On a more practical level, Esprit, Race and Brite have been in progress long enough to have generated both a more sophisticated understanding and practical experience of what cooperative R&D entails. Esprit, of course, was tailor-made to the IT industry's perceptions and demands. The twelve founding members of the initial Round Table have continued to influence the programme's shape and direction and find its framework attractive. The clarity with which Esprit and Brite have approached contractual matters is also considered by many to be useful. When companies participate in several projects with a number of collaborators, they need a degree of standardization and predictability about the conditions of collaboration. The Commission has gone some way to providing these through its detailed guidelines and standard contract.

The experience of small and medium-sized enterprises (SMEs) has been somewhat different. For many of these, the major problem with European collaboration has been a question of access. Esprit, for example, has been viewed by many SMEs in terms of the emergence of a core of decision-makers from the large companies, national administrations and the Commission. Their continued contact with each other has developed into and reinforced a relatively closed world, with its own internal consensus about the problems to be addressed and the strategies to be adopted. Brite, on the other hand, expands its net more widely. But even so it must be noted that, rightly or wrongly, Community policy for high technology has not yet had as an explicit objective the systematic promotion of the involvement of SMEs.[16]

Where access to particular programmes has been achieved, the relative lack of resources of smaller companies in terms of finance and contacts has tended to exacerbate the existing difficulties associated with European collaboration. The finding of partners is an obvious example, with many companies reduced to random telephone calls across Europe despite the services of the so-called marriage bureaux. The extra costs associated with collaboration may prove too much for smaller firms, which may be reluctant to release senior staff (often their scarcest resource) for what might turn out to be unproductive efforts for which the award of a contract is uncertain or the availability and timing of funding is open to doubt. Bureaucratic procedures and delays, which the Commission has sought to minimize, can act as further deterrents. Despite these difficulties, some smaller companies have found European collaboration a fruitful experience, not least because of the doors it has opened to them in terms of personal contacts and the potential for future associations.

*The future*
As mentioned above, these various Community initiatives fall under the umbrella of the European Community's Framework Programme. The Commission is currently negotiating the Second Framework Programme with member states, but at the time of writing the situation does not look promising. The Commission initially suggested a funding level of 10.3 billion ecus, but in July 1986 pressure from larger member states reduced the figure to 7.7 billion. This is still not low enough to satisfy the British, French and German governments, especially given the other pressures on Community expenditure, to which these three countries are the largest contributors. The smaller member states, and particularly the Mediterranean countries, are keen to support the programme. Council meetings in December 1986 failed to reach any agreement and forced the Commission into making a further compromise offer of an interim 3.5 billion ecus plan, with funding gradually increasing over time.

The reluctance of the British, French and German governments to give generous support to the Framework Programme has major implications for the effective continuation of Esprit, Brite and Race, even though many of the projects have been agreed in principle. To some it also seems rather perverse, in so far as British, French and German companies stand to benefit from the projects.

65

Unfortunately, Community initiatives in this field cannot be de-coupled from the rest of the Community's activities, nor from the pressures on national R&D budgets with which Community programmes have to jostle for support.

# 4

# THE WIDER
# EUROPEAN CONTEXT

The debate about technological collaboration in Western Europe has thrown up two major questions: What frameworks are most conducive to concrete results? And where can the motive forces be generated? Chapters 2 and 3 have focused on a range of examples, some within the Community, others through less institutionalized consortia but each dealing with particular sectors or products. But this covers only part of the picture. There is an emerging consensus that, unless industrialists themselves are persuaded of the relevance of each collaboration, little of durable economic and commercial importance will be achieved. It follows that the role of private financing is crucial, whether in tandem with public funding or as the primary source of investment in technology.

Equally, as the earlier analysis demonstrates, the success of collaborative ventures depends on achieving an appropriate blend of complementary assets and interests. This means that no single formula is likely to suit all cases. We should instead expect to find a diverse range of collaborative patterns (see Tables 1.13 and 1.14). And indeed we should not be surprised that some ventures include American or Japanese partners as well as or instead of other Europeans. As many industrialists argue, what they are interested in is 'horses for courses', and what they look to governments and the Community to provide is a framework and instruments which will aid them, both in their search for partners and in the consummation of their collaborative ventures. The framework and instruments which are relevant range from the general approach to the specifics of legal parameters, tax regimes, market conditions and so on. This chapter explores these wider dimensions: from the efforts of the European Commission to promote a broad concept of a European Technology Community; through the Eureka initiative; to the development of industrial and financial networks.

**European Technology Community**

The concept of a European Technology Community (ETC) centred on the EC is still with us. Davignon's successor, Karl-Heinz Narjes, relaunched it in June 1985.[1] His idea was to provide not only a tighter conceptual framework for the various strands of EC activity, but an effective bridge between national, Community and extra-Community R&D activities. A memorandum outlined a number of different activities that might be undertaken under the umbrella of the ETC. These ranged from generic technology programmes, such as Esprit, to the activities of the European Space Agency and the development of major large-scale scientific research initiatives such as CERN at Geneva and the JET project at Culham (not covered in this paper).

Narjes identified a number of different collaborative models from the flexible groupings of Esprit and Brite to the more formal agreements signed at government level in Euratom. Small and medium enterprises would receive special attention since they tended to be overlooked in strictly intergovernmental schemes of cooperation, and the ETC would provide a framework for the horizontal coordination of research initiatives, standardization of efforts, dissemination of results and the stimulation of future activities.

Finance from the Community budget would operate according to a multiannual framework programme (See Chapter 3) but the details and methods of implementation would rest more squarely with the Commission. Member states would participate in ETC programmes on a 'variable geometry' basis across ten major policy areas: information technology and its main applications, biotechnology, new materials, lasers and optics, large scientific instruments, broadband telecommunications, new generation means of transport, space, marine environment, and education and training technologies.

The ETC formed part of the discussions in the intergovernmental meetings on the reform of the Treaty of Rome, which were initiated by the European Council in Milan in June 1985. Although the Commission did not succeed in its main objective – to supersede the Eureka initiative (see below) – it did acquire an improved legal standing for its industrial R&D activities. The Single European Act has now specified the EC's role in relation to technology and provided it with powers to strengthen European industry. The detailed planning is of course still subject to the constraints of budgetary decisions and to other factors such as market liberalization and so on.[2]

### Eureka

Three weeks after the Commission published its memorandum on the ETC, the French Minister for Technology, M. Curien, hosted the first Eureka Conference of Ministers in Paris. Launched in April 1985, the European Research Coordinating Agency, or Eureka, was a French-inspired initiative in direct response to the US Strategic Defense Initiative (SDI), or Star Wars programme. The reaction of European governments to SDI, and to the Pentagon's attempts to recruit research expertise from European firms and universities, varied. Britain tried to acquire a guarantee of SDI contracts worth $1.5 billion, and its criticism was therefore muted. But the German Foreign Minister, Hans-Dietrich Genscher, was adamant that his country would not follow suit. He was quick to lend his government's active support to the Eureka initiative, making it clear that he shared the French distrust of the Star Wars concept, and was anxious not to see Germany's best brains diverted to SDI.

While the French press presented Eureka in defence terms as France's answer to Star Wars, President Mitterrand's aim was also to counter the commercial spin-off which it was believed would flow out of the SDI initiative. Thus Eureka was presented as an essential civilian programme, complementary to SDI and, for some, competitive with it.

It thus attracted the support of many European governments irrespective of their SDI stance. Its timing moreover neatly pre-empted the Commission's ETC concept and its implicit bid for leadership of Eureka, thereby ensuring that this new proposal for European technological collaboration was pursued individually by the participating governments, including many from outside the EC. At this point the British government also became interested and from June 1985 onwards took an uncharacteristically prominent role in promoting the concept.

By June 1985 Eureka had become a key theme at the European Council meeting in Milan. Endorsing the initiative in principle, ministers agreed to meet the following month in Paris. The first agreement under the Eureka umbrella was one between the French defence and electronics group, Matra, and Norsk Data of Norway to cooperate in developing a European high-performance or 'super' computer. It was with this agreement that Eureka was formally launched in June 1985.

At the July meeting in Paris discussion centred on the White Paper 'Technological Renaissance in Europe', put forward by the French.[3] Five priority areas for Eureka activities were suggested: information technology, robotics, communications, biotechnology and new materials. Each was encompassed within a suitable acronym. Thus EUROMATIQUE covered activities involving large computers, paralleled architecture, intelligence and expert systems, silicon materials and gallium arsenide circuits. EUROBOT dealt with third-generation robots, automated factories and lasers; EUROCOM with broadband communications network equipment and research networks; EUROMAT with ceramic turbines and high-speed trains; and EUROBIO with different applications of biotechnology. For each of these areas France provided information on the potential nature of the projects, possible work programmes and interested industrial partners. Priority was given to French firms and to certain large British and German firms. Britain proposed three further programmes: namely, EUROFAC, for the integration of high technologies in factories; EUROHOME for the adaptation of technologies in the home; and EUROTYPE, which aimed to accelerate the process of formulating European standards, to establish tax incentives for the creation of 'European' firms and to develop a policy in relation to public procurement markets. While the emphasis here was on industrialists defining the scope of specific projects, governments were also felt to have a role to play alongside companies and financiers. Some items, such as the EUROTYPE proposals, seemed appropriate for the European Commission to develop within the EC framework.

A second meeting on Eureka was held in Hanover under German presidency in November 1985. Here the 18 participating countries (now including Turkey) and the European Commission formally adopted the Eureka Charter, or declaration of principles, and published a list of multinational projects. The Charter provides the programme with a legal basis. It defined Eureka as a forum within which companies could cooperate across borders aided by the gradual abolition of national barriers and, in time, by a genuine common market. The emphasis lay on 'post-basic research', i.e., the stimulation of work by European firms and research centres in pursuit of rapidly marketable products. The sectors agreed upon were information technology and telecommunications, lasers, robotics, biotechnology, materials, manufacturing, marine technology, environmental protection, computer-assisted production and transport technologies. No indication of relative priorities or values was given. Ten projects were agreed upon, a somewhat mixed bag in which some hardy perennials of European technology reappeared. But there were also some genuinely new collaborations, such as an agreement between Olivetti, Acorn and Thomson to collaborate on developing a European standard for personal and educational microcomputers, work on compact vector computers for high-speed calculations shared between Matra and Norsk Data, and a European research computer network involving France, Germany, Austria, Finland, Sweden, Switzerland, the Netherlands and the European Commission.

A further meeting in January 1986 in London, under British presidency, increased the number of projects and agreed in outline the shape of the Eureka secretariat. This was to comprise seven seconded officials, including one from the Commission. It was to act as a clearing house, circulating information about the projects agreed on to government and industry, and perhaps to monitor results as the projects came on stream. No right of initiative was conferred upon it. Indeed it was not to intervene even to the extent of assembling partners for the different projects. The secretariat's location was decided in June. France had proposed Strasbourg, and Saarbrücken and Geneva had been put forward as possibilities, but in the event Brussels provided the most convenient solution. The June 1986 meeting also resulted in agreement on 60 further projects (an illustrative list of Eureka projects appears in Table 4.1). At the December 1986 meeting in Stockholm, a further 37 projects representing 730 mecus (£525m) were agreed on, including one between Thomson and SGS (the Italian semiconductor manufac-

## Table 4.1 Illustrative list of Eureka projects

| Title of project | Partners from | Objective | Cost/length |
|---|---|---|---|
| Eurocim | France, Spain; interest expressed by Italy | Automated factory to manufacture electronic cards | 30 mecus; 5 years |
| Cerise | France, Luxembourg | European centre for synthesizing computer images | 8.5 mecus; 5 years |
| ES2 | Joint venture: Belgium, France, W. Germany, UK, possibly Finland (and others) | Production of integrated circuits using direct impression silicon | 3 years |
| Gallium arsenide | France, UK | Processes for monolithic integrated circuits for microwaves from gallium arsenide | 60 mecus; 3 years |
| Mobile robot | France, Spain; interest from W. Germany and Switzerland | Third generation robots for public safety | 100 mecus; 6 years |
| Expert system | Norway, France | To handle breakdowns in production units and their safety | 30 mecus; 4 years |
| East (Eureka Advance Software Technology) | Denmark, Finland, France; interest from UK, Italy, Sweden, Switzerland | The development of software workshops | 110 mecus; 6 years |
| Paradi | Belgium, France; interest from Italy, Spain, W. Germany and Switzerland | System of automatic production management using artificial intelligence | 30 mecus; 6 years |
| Diane | France, Spain; interest from W. Germany | Automatic integrated system for neutronography | 15 mecus; 4 years |
| Disposal of Chemical waste | Belgium, France; interest from Italy and the Netherlands | To use high-powered lasers to detect and destroy impurities | 9 mecus; 5 years |
| GTO thyristors | France, UK | To use GTO thyristors with systems of iron traction | 20 mecus; 2 years |
| Chromium salt substitutes | Austria, Greece and Spain | To use aluminium in the treatment of leather | 2.5 mecus; 3 years |

Table 4.1 concluded

| Title of project | Partners from | Objective | Cost/length |
| --- | --- | --- | --- |
| Galemo 2000 | Denmark, Spain; interest from France | Equipment for automatic medical diagnosis based on new sensors and artificial intelligence | 60 mecus; 5 years |
| Vehicle noise identification | Belgium, W. Germany; interest from Sweden and UK | A new, more precise and automatic method | 1.5 mecus; 4 years |
| Apex | France, Italy; interest from Belgium and UK | European information exchange on the aerospace industry | 30 mecus; 5 years |
| New engine material | France, Italy | Ceramics and metals | 25 mecus; 5 years |

*Note*: These particular projects were all agreed upon in London, 22/23 January, 1986.

turer) to develop a new generation four-megabit Eprom (Erasable Programmable Read-Only Memory) chip.

The extent to which Eureka should be publicly financed was early on the subject of some debate. The British, Spanish and Swiss clearly favoured private financing by companies and venture capitalists, and stressed the importance of attracting private capital. The French government indicated it was prepared to allocate 1 billion French francs, and the German government offered a contribution of DM 300m. The final agreement was that Eureka would receive 'suitable support by the governments of the participating countries and by the European Community' and 'the enterprise institutions participating in a Eureka project will finance the project from their own funds, the capital market and any public funds made available to them.'[4]

Differences of opinion about funding do cause problems. In the absence of collective funding either through Eureka or the EC budget, investment depends on national rules for public expenditure and the local availability of private capital. Although this may make perfectly good economic and administrative sense, it has caused some difficulties for firms, especially when would-be partners have had mismatching resource bases. Nonetheless, the Eureka forum has been encouraged to engage investors directly in the debate. At the Stockholm meeting in December 1986 industrialists also participated.

One constructive outcome of the early Eureka discussions was the establishment of criteria by which projects could qualify for the Eureka label, although the mechanism for granting it, and its consequent status and usefulness, remained vague. Some agreement was reached on information exchanges about projects and proposals, but again it would seem that technology transfer as such will not flow from participation in Eureka, and will be subject to the normal commercial conditions. It is therefore difficult to gauge the precise advantages accruing to those member states participating in only a small number of projects. Behind this lies a broad and difficult question of what counts as a 'European company'. Just as Esprit had ducked this issue by admitting IBM to token membership, so in Eureka it was conveniently left to the participating governments to adopt particular projects for Eureka badging.

The negotiations on Eureka have clearly left a number of issues unresolved. Most important, perhaps, is the priority to be accorded to the different technological sectors and the procedures to be adopted for project selection. A closer examination of the projects points to a number of factors.[5] Major differences in scale exist. Some projects have a clear basic research context while others fall into stages of the cycle from research to exploitation. Overlap occurs with existing Community programmes and the distribution of projects between member states is fairly uneven. The 'variable geometry' approach, however, provides for greater flexibility than perhaps the EC offers. It has certainly met with a warm response from European countries outside the EC. But some would argue that similar results could have been largely accommodated within the existing COST framework, though COST has not had so high a political profile.

### Internal Market

A recurrent theme in the context of Eureka, as in all discussions of European technology, concerns the market conditions. Eureka states have allocated to the Commission an infrastructural role in defining ways of eliminating some of the constraints currently impeding collaboration at the European level. These centre on the absence of a full internal market, aptly reflected in the underdevelopment of the common legal structure, and the absence of some key European standards or a unified European venture capital market. While EC member states have expressed their commitment to the completion of a European internal market by 1992, progress on the key technological issues needs to be much faster. In the area of public purchasing, for example, the Commission has had little success in persuading governments and other public sector agencies to consider tenders from companies outside their immediate national boundaries. EEC directives dating back to 1971 require Community-wide advertising of public sector contracts, but even now only a very small proportion of these involve cross-national interests. The Commission has suggested that within the telecommunications sector governments should adopt open tendering. For other kinds of equipment the Commission has recommended a gradual opening up of national procurement markets, while the French government has suggested an initial phase during which 10 per cent of spending would be open to foreign suppliers.

**Industry-to-industry initiatives**
At the industrial level, meanwhile, companies have begun to take their own steps towards collaboration. These have varied from formal joint ventures in research and product development to informal agreements to cooperate over technical standards.[6] To date, the major axis of European industrial alliances has remained transatlantic. In the telecommunications sector, for example, both Philips (the Netherlands) and Olivetti (Italy) have formed close links with AT&T. IBM has sought to establish ties with West European national telecommunications authorities, while West Germany's Siemens has been openly dismissive of an all-European strategy in telecommunications manufacturing. Nevertheless, a modest intra-European trend of collaboration is beginning to emerge (see Table 1.13). Wholly European-oriented agreements to date include the 1984 alliance between CGE (France) and the broadly based holding company Société Générale de Belgique to foster high-tech developments in telecommunications, and the 1985 accord between CIT Alcatel (France), Italtel (Italy), Siemens (West Germany) and Plessey (UK) over technical cooperation in new exchanges and transmis-

sion techniques that are designed to pave the way for the joint building of future public telephone switching systems. Examples of European collaboration in computing include the 1984 Racal (UK) and Norsk Data (Norway) joint venture for computer systems to facilitate the development of artificial intelligence, the 1985 agreement between Thomson (France) and Cambridge Instruments (UK) in the field of high-speed submicron lithography, and the 1986 agreement between Thomson and GEC (UK) for a five-year programme to develop application specific integrated circuits.

Better publicized, perhaps, is the Munich-based joint research centre set up by Bull (France), Siemens (West Germany) and ICL (UK) in 1984 to promote the development of new-generation computers. Philips and Siemens have meanwhile been cooperating in long-lead R&D since 1982. In 1984 this collaboration branched out with the launching of the so-called megaproject, which had considerable financial support from the West German and Dutch governments.

A more recent approach to the concept of European industrial collaboration was the formation of the European Silicon Structures (ES2) microchip venture, announced in September 1985. Established as a purely European operation in terms of its sources of finance, senior management, choice of location and marketing goals, ES2 aims to use advanced design and production technology for the cheap and efficient manufacture of small quantities of custom chips. Incorporated in Luxembourg, it has located its headquarters in West Germany, developed its design technology in the UK and based its production facilities in France.

**Private financing of European collaboration**
The current spate of collaborative activities, and the emergence of Eureka in particular, has raised the issue of how best to finance such initiatives. One way governments can and have shown encouragement is through direct support, but this clearly increases public expenditure, which is subject to constraints in nearly all the European countries concerned. An alternative might be public support in the form of loans and equity designed to achieve a commercial return and executed through, for example, the European Investment Bank (EIB). Equally important, for the future at least, is the role to be played by the private sector. While large

companies tend to finance collaborative ventures out of their own funds, small and medium-sized firms have a need for external funding, particularly in the form of venture capital.

The European venture capital industry is still very much in its infancy. The most advanced venture capital market in Europe is that of the UK, but activities in many other West European countries are beginning to take off, and the amount of venture capital available within Europe is no longer a problem. Recent estimates have put the figure within the region of 5,000 to 7,000 mecus.[7] A breakdown of the industrial sectors within the EC receiving risk investment suggests that high-tech companies have had a fair share of the venture capital disbursed. Computers and related products, for example, account for 18.8 per cent of European venture capital investment; equipment and machinery account for 12.9 per cent; electronic components 10.9 per cent; communications (including telecommunications and transportation) 4.8 per cent and biotechnology (including genetic engineering) 4.5 per cent.[8]

But the European venture capital industry is not without its difficulties. One major problem is the relative dearth across Europe of venture capitalists with sufficient experience and/or training to manage large numbers of transnational ventures effectively. Second, although funds are nominally available for venture capital throughout Europe, the general lack of sufficiently good quality projects from young companies requesting investment means that a large proportion of funds are being channelled into mature companies that require development capital. Only 12 per cent of syndicates, moreover, involve transnational investment. These facts indicate the particular problems faced by small and medium-sized companies in acquiring venture capital funding. Lacking the international structure of their larger counterparts, they are doubly disadvantaged in terms of the constraints inherent in a fragmented capital market at the European level.

## The European Venture Capital Association and Community schemes

In an effort to overcome some of these problems and to complement initiatives at the national level, a number of developments are currently under way to reinforce the involvement of venture capital organizations in the broad European technology efforts. Foremost among these has been the establishment of the European Venture Capital Association (EVCA). Backed by the Community, it aims to facilitate discussion and study of the management and investment of venture capital and to promote the development of a European capital market. Part of its success to date was reflected in the Eureka communiqué of 1986, which recognized the role played by venture capital in developing Europe's technology. The EVCA has also been active in promoting the role of venture capital within the framework of the European Community. A number of schemes designed to encourage cross-border syndication are currently under discussion, although only one – the Venture Consort Scheme – has so far been implemented. Set up as a pilot programme in collaboration with the EVCA, the Venture Consort Scheme is aimed specifically at small and medium-sized enterprises. Projects involve a maximum of 30 per cent Community financing and should wherever possible complement other Community policies and programmes. The scheme was initiated about one year ago, and 17 out of 25 projects have so far received approval. Two of these were subsequently withdrawn by the investors' syndicates, but the rest have received a total funding of 2.8 mecus.

Two other proposals currently on the table are the NCI IV and the Eurotech Capital and Insurance Scheme. The concept of the New Community Instruments (NCI) as a financial mechanism was introduced in 1979. Three models have been approved to date. The fourth, NCI IV, proposed by the Commission in June 1985, is intended to help finance investments in small and medium-sized companies concerned with the application of new technologies and innovations. The Eurotech scheme, by contrast, is designed to encourage companies to develop ideas emerging from Community programmes at a very early stage.[9]

**Institutional and tax incentives**

Other institutional incentives which would help the financing problem include a modification of the, to date, rather conservative guidelines surrounding the EIB's operations, or even the creation of a new European 'technological risk fund'. Communication links between the providers and seekers of venture capital funds are also important and the link that has been formed between the EVCA and the Eureka secretariat is a first step in this direction. Tax incentives meanwhile need not necessarily involve a loss of public revenue if sufficient extra activity is generated. Examples of the kind which might operate successfully at the European level (requiring the cooperation of national governments) include European investment incentives for individuals through unit trusts and the development of European enterprise zones.

## Continuing problems in European collaboration

### The role of the state

Recent experience in European cooperation has served to highlight a number of major issues. The Eureka initiative, for example, revealed considerable differences between West European governments as to the most appropriate role of the state. Here France and West Germany initially agreed that Eureka would require specific funding from governmental budgets, while the British government insisted that the venture be financed from private markets and/or existing support schemes. Inconsistencies emerged when, under pressure from British companies, the UK government acquired 'more' money from the Treasury for a special contingency fund. Meanwhile, the West German government was having to deal with hostility from its own Finance Ministry, which had taken its lead from the tough line originally adopted by the UK Treasury. Similarly, in responding to the Commission's proposals for a European Technology Community, both West Germany and the UK focused on the need for budgetary discipline while France argued for an increase in expenditure levels.

These differences in national stance are heightened by strategic considerations, particularly in the IT sector, where the distinction between the products destined for civilian applications and those for military purposes is becoming increasingly blurred. The great interest and enthusiasm demonstrated during the early stages of the Eureka discussions by both France and West Germany is not unrelated to their respective approaches to the notion of strategic dependence on the USA. Both are also anxious to avoid situations in which US foreign policy dictates the use, transfer and sale of technology through licence controls. Even Britain is having problems in gaining access to US technology, particularly in the heavily classified SDI area, while American attempts to exert extraterritorial control over re-exports of US-manufactured high-tech equipment continue to cause major diplomatic friction. It was significant that increasing British interest in Eureka as the initiative was elaborated reflected heightened awareness of the problems of technological overdependence on the USA.

### A European forum?

Such considerations inevitably raise the question of what constitutes the most appropriate forum, politically and technically, for collaboration. Debate lingers over the relative merits of Western Europe versus the United States and Japan. Political concerns over the implications of Western Europe's technology gap, together with the strategic considerations inherent in the policies of certain West European states, militate in favour of some kind of European forum. The bias in industrial cooperation, however, has in the past leaned more towards the transatlantic axis. At times this has reflected the weaknesses of Western Europe as much as the attractions of its competitors. Both Olivetti and Philips, for example, sought European partners before concluding their respective deals with AT&T, but found little basis for any real agreement. The lack of complementary products and technology among West European competitors has been a major problem. Equally important, though, is the reluctance of European companies so far to surrender their privileged positions at home. Even where the level of industrial commitment to a European framework has been much more overt – as in the case of the Philips and Siemens megaproject – extra-European agreements have had to be concluded during the course of the project in order to acquire the relevant expertise and know-how.[10] Given the location of much relevant expertise outside Western Europe and the potential access to new markets which transatlantic agreements might offer, it is not altogether surprising that during the second half of 1985 European companies in the telecommunications sector negotiated or discussed some 17 arrangements with US or Japanese companies, compared with only 7 within Europe.[11]

### The European Community v. Eureka?

But even when a specifically European forum is desirable, problems arise. From the European Commission's point of view the advantage and potential of the EC dimension are clear. Western Europe's weaknesses are perceived to arise out of its fragmented markets and uncoordinated strategies. Potentially, the Community framework offers the opportunity to unify the market, while, for members and non-members of the EC alike, the COST framework provides the same kind of flexibility as Eureka.

Yet the European Community poses a problem in terms of its membership. On the one hand, certain West European states and prominent companies such as Ericsson of Sweden fall outside its jurisdiction (although there has been a spate of interest in renewing EC/EFTA research cooperation agreements); on the other hand, increasing tensions are being generated by the Community's expansion. With the accession of Spain and Portugal in 1986, regional, industrial and technological disparities between member states plunged the Community into a state of flux with respect to its purpose, direction and general mode of operation. Such tensions threaten the long-term security of Community programmes, and it is important that they are not seen as pandering to special interest groups either among, or within, nations.

The usefulness of the Commission as a political agency and arbitrator, however, should not be underestimated. The EC-IBM settlement of August 1984 is a good example of its power. This requires IBM to adhere to four basic points. Within four months of announcing a new computer, IBM must now provide sufficient interface information to enable competing companies within the Community to attach both hard and software products of their design to the System/370. Second, IBM is required to disclose adequate and timely technical details of the Systems Network Architecture for the System/370. Third, it must offer its System/370 CPUs within the Community without main memory or with only the necessary capacity for testing. Finally, IBM is to continue its efforts to match its Systems Network Architecture to the Open Systems Interconnection (OSI) standard used by other West European companies.

The effects of the agreement are threefold. First, it improves the position of both users and competitors, since the earlier availability of interface information potentially allows competitors the opportunity to market their products simultaneously with an IBM introduction. Second, an element of certainty has been introduced in so far as potential buyers will have more assurance that other manufacturers' equipment will be IBM-compatible. Third, IBM's agreement to allow the purchase of mainframe computers without data storage memory gives their customers the option to buy rival main memory at a lower price.[12]

Although the EC-IBM settlement is unlikely to reduce IBM's dominance in the European computer industry, it has achieved a number of first-time concessions from IBM. Most importantly, and in the Commission's favour, it represents the *first* time that any 'governmental' entity has persuaded IBM to adhere to a firm timetable for information disclosure, or established formal procedures whereby IBM's business practices can be reviewed by an official body.

The Commission's success in negotiating with IBM, however, is tempered by its position with regard to West European intergovernmental politics. Thus, a situation has arisen in which two separate intergovernmental frameworks – the European Community and Eureka – have emerged for European collaboration. The Community may not be the most appropriate forum for every case of European collaboration, and so alternative frameworks should offer quite clear and distinct advantages. For many in industry, however, the differences between Eureka and the Community are not immediately apparent. Ostensibly, programmes such as Esprit and Brite deal with the pre-competitive aspects of basic research, while Eureka's remit is to focus on more downstream product- and market-oriented projects within the context of a wider membership. Such differences, however, are not so clearly delineated in practice. Since the line distinguishing the pre-competitive from the competitive cannot be accurately drawn, a certain amount of overlap occurs both in the nature of the research and the topics that are covered. Similarly, plans for Esprit 2, which provide the potential for agreements to be drawn up with EFTA countries, would seem to narrow the gap between the two frameworks even further.[13]

**Conclusions**

European collaboration in the 1980s continues to be directly and indirectly afflicted by intergovernmental rivalries among national states and with the European Community. A qualitative change has nevertheless occurred at the industrial level, where what might be termed a technological 'Community' is in the process of emerging.

Debate continues as to the most appropriate framework for collaborative activities, but recently the European Community has proved to be a much more effective forum than hitherto. Access to the European collaboration programmes in general, and to those in the IT sector in particular, has so far been relatively limited, while inadequate political commitment on the part of the national governments and some of their industries has constrained the infrastructural developments necessary if more effective collaboration at the European level is to be realized.

# 5

# CONCLUSIONS

We now return to the central question of this paper: why should European governments, and especially the British government, actively seek to promote technological collaboration between *European* firms and institutions?

The case for technological collaboration itself is clear. In an increasing number of high-tech areas the costs of keeping pace with current technological developments, combined with a shortening product life-cycle, make a strategy of sharing costs and risks a very attractive one. In addition, technological convergence means that no firm competing at world market levels can any longer rely upon having at its fingertips the range of skills and competence necessary for modern product development; so collaboration may become the only viable way forward. To develop new skills in-house takes time and resources, and risks under-utilization of an expensive asset. To buy them in, either from contract research establishments (as happens in biotechnology) or from other firms possessing the necessary 'complementarity' of assets and markets, becomes an increasingly attractive option, particularly where such a relationship brings a simultaneous sharing of costs and risks.

The key issue, however, is that of complementarity. If two firms are to link together successfully in a joint venture, they need a complementarity not only of technical know-how and resources, but also of markets. The strategic alliances that are effective in these circumstances are those with pay-offs on both sides. The price of technological know-how may well be facilitating market entry for others. Where markets are complementary, as for example with

Olivetti's office equipment markets and AT&T's telecommunications enterprise, the marriage makes sense. In contrast, a marriage such as the unfortunate Dunlop-Pirelli partnership in the early 1970s, in which the two partners were competitors in both technology and markets, has little solid base of complementarities to build upon.

But does *European* collaboration make sense? The degree to which in the past few years European firms have been seeking partners in high-technology products is logical and sensible. That said, is there any merit in these partners being European rather than Japanese or American firms? On the face of it, for both technological and market reasons, alliances with either Japanese or American firms might seem more appropriate. Although this paper disputes the facile concept of the technology gap, by pointing to the diversity of technological resources and capabilities from country to country, there is no denying that European firms have been at some disadvantage in the broad area of information technology in relation to their competitors in the USA and Japan. Firms in these two countries have the technology the Europeans need, and, often, a link-up with them provides much-needed access to Japanese or American markets, which for one reason or another may be closed if there is no indigenous partner. The logical alliances might therefore be with Japanese or US firms rather than with European competitors, and the trend has been in this direction. Witness, for example, ICL's and Siemens's links with Fujitsu, the Philips joint venture with AT&T and Italtel's links with GTE. These are strategic alliances, marrying complementary resources with pay-offs for each side in terms of access to technology and/or access to markets.

It would be wrong to suggest that such complementarities do not exist between European partners. Given the diversity of technological endowments within Europe, there are always likely to be some productive possibilities. Likewise, although the existence of the EC should mean little problem of market entry, in practice many high-tech markets have been fragmented by oligopolistic management on the one hand, and by language and regulatory and public purchasing barriers on the other. ICL's link with Siemens and Bull is as much about access to European markets as it is about joint product development, as indeed is CGE's recent link-up with ITT.

When collaboration is seen in this light, is there any need to invest public money in the process? Like it or no, European programmes such as Esprit and the Eureka initiative are about putting public money into the process of collaboration. Over its first four-year span of 1984–8, the Esprit programme is set to spend about 750 mecus, with, of course, parallel industrial funding; Race is set to cost some 50 mecus per annum in its present phase, and more later. All told, Community support for collaborative R&D, the essence of which is cross-border collaboration between industries and/or universities and research institutes, currently amounts to about 900 mecus a year. Under the new Framework Programme the Commission hopes to push this up to 1.9 billion ecus a year, which is small in comparison with the sum of national support programmes: Britain, France and West Germany are each spending upwards of 2 billion ecus a year supporting R&D, and 500 mecus a year on electronics alone. It is even smaller when compared to the sums being poured into R&D in the USA, much of it via Department of Defense programmes. Nevertheless, as one corporate commentator remarked apropos of the Eureka initiative, 'I cannot understand why governments should wish to subsidize such programmes. Many of the projects would have gone ahead under their own steam. Those that would not are probably not worth pursuing. If only the governments involved would put the equivalent sums into education and training, which is the area where Europe really lags behind the US and Japan, the benefit would be so much greater.'[1]

The contrary view is perhaps best summed up by Sir Michael Butler, until 1985 Britain's Permanent Representative to the European Community. Writing in *The Financial Times* in the wake of the Westland affair, he disputed the notion that it does not matter if European companies become technologically dependent upon US or Japanese multinationals. 'The multinationals are in Europe to promote their parent companies' strategy for gaining world market share,' he argued. 'Once they have knocked out or taken over the European competition, they will be free to shift the balance of their investment in plant and research towards home ... European industry in other fields will suffer. Still more profits, investment and research will flow home ... The basic idea behind Eureka, that European companies need to cooperate in order to survive, is right'.[2] Rob Wilmot, the former MD of ICL and a co-founder of ES2, argues: 'Many Europeans still do not understand the fierceness and implications of the battle (taking place between the USA and Japan).' In particular he is afraid that deregulatory pressures to open up markets, necessary as this step is to European competitive-ness, will liberalize European markets before European companies are ready to compete. 'The pressure on already fragile national suppliers is just the strategic gap our competitors have been waiting for.'[3]

Joan Pearce and John Sutton take a somewhat different line. They reject the implicit protectionism of some commentators. 'Economic analysis points to the desirability of convergence on a lower rather than a higher level of protection. This amounts to advocating that some member states which are feeling international competition most keenly should reduce their protection. Policy-makers say this is a counsel of perfection. They are perhaps more influenced by immediate political imperatives than by the economic costs which emerge only over some time.' But they also see collaboration as a way forward. 'If policy-makers wish (the development of the European industrial base) to occur, there is much they can do to facilitate it. *Financial support for collaborative ventures – for exam-ple, through programmes like Esprit – can encourage firms to pursue cooperation which they might not otherwise consider*. Firms, them-selves, however, maintain that far more important is the removal of internal barriers and the revision of Community and national laws and regulations so as to make it easier to establish and operate European companies.'[4]

The sentence italicized in this last quotation is the key to the various programmes discussed in Chapters 2, 3 and 4 aimed at promoting European collaboration. But it has also to be asked what benefit is derived from such cooperation and, ultimately, whether the benefits justify the costs.

### The benefits gained from European collaboration

There are various benefits that Europe gains from collaboration. Loosely, they can be defined as economic benefits and political benefits, although the categories as we shall see are not exclusive, and what purports to be an economic benefit often turns out to be mainly political and vice versa.

One set of economic benefits which Europe, and more specifically the EC, gains from promoting cooperation comes into a category which economists label 'externalities' – benefits attributable to a line of action which accrue not to one firm or individual but to society as a whole. Because they do not accrue to individual firms, they do not show up in profits; hence, left to themselves, firms can take decisions alien to the public interest. This constitutes what is known as 'market failure', and it is an argument that has long been used to justify government intervention to adjust market prices via taxes and/or subsidies.

## The improvement of information flows

Any firm contemplating collaboration needs detailed information to help it identify potential partners. There is, however, often a natural bias towards firms that are known to each other – i.e., the 'better the devil you know' syndrome. The tendency to treat the European, US and Far Eastern markets as separate entities, and for European firms to run European operations from their home base, means that cross-licensing and marketing arrangements are *more likely* to be biased towards non-European than European firms. At the very least, therefore, there is something to be said for a mechanism which encourages a wider search for European opportunities, and both Esprit and Eureka have been successful in forging links where the participants admit that lack of knowledge had inhibited earlier contacts.

The same argument applies to links between firms and academic/technological research institutes. Where such channels do exist – for example in West Germany through the joint industry/government-funded Frauenhofer research institutes – they are usually nationally based and have little contact with research centres in other European countries. These barriers are, however, breaking down. It is notable, for example, that the European Federation for Biotechnology, founded in 1978 as a society linking industry, research institutes and universities, provided much of the impetus for the EC biotechnology programmes; and the Biomolecular Engineering Programme (Bep) is a striking example of how successful programmes based on the exchange of ideas, information and personnel can be. It is interesting, too, that the industrial/academic links established through Esprit are deemed to have been especially valuable.

## The promotion of R&D

It has long been recognized by economists that many firms are dissuaded from putting resources into R&D because they cannot be sure that they will be able to profit directly from such expenditures.

This applies particularly to basic research, most of the results of which are not patentable, and the argument has long been the justification for government funding of basic R&D. But as industry pushes its R&D increasingly upstream towards more basic research, there is a growing grey area of 'pre-competitive research'. This includes, for example, developments in the tools and techniques for production, such as submicron technologies. Here the work involved is often not patentable or otherwise appropriable as intellectual property, but it is equally dependent on the knowledge and experience of those involved in the research. If these people move to another firm, then the firm undertaking the original research has no way of preventing its rival from exploiting it, a factor which in itself can be a major disincentive to undertake R&D in the first place.

Cooperative R&D overcomes these problems. The research is undertaken jointly and the results are freely available to all members of the research club, who are at liberty to exploit them. From the firm's point of view the club may have another advantage: a sharing of risk. Any new project involves an element of technological risk – it may not be able to achieve the technological goals it set out with – but in addition there is a strategic risk, namely, that of discovering that you have put all your eggs in one basket and your competitors have put theirs into a different one. The great advantage of collaborative agreements such as Esprit or Race is that they lock your competitors into the same game! Research clubs may therefore serve to encourage firms to spend more on R&D than they would do otherwise. Given Europe's relatively low spending on industrial R&D, this can only be beneficial.

There is another category of economic factors favouring European collaboration, which economists might describe as a 'second best' rationale.[5] If the 'first best' solution (which economists would see as a fully fledged free-trade world) is not achievable, collaboration, though not perfect, may be the next best option. This argument is especially relevant to the problems of competition with the USA and Japan and to the imperfections of European markets.

*Countering US and Japanese protectionism*
The world is not perfect. The USA protects and promotes its high-technology industries via huge subsidies from the Department of

Defense, the Buy-American Act and all kinds of other non-tariff barriers. The Japanese likewise benefit from organizational assistance and subsidies via MITI, and from numerous methods (not least the Japanese language) of keeping foreign exports out of their market, all embedded in a strategic economic nationalism. The straight tit-for-tat argument justifies some protection, but subsidy plus collaboration offers a more constructive response than just straight tariff protection. It is an acknowledgment that in the modern world the individual nation states of Europe have little clout against the huge economic power wielded by the USA and Japan, countries which operate as *nation* states, with a single set of economic and industrial policies. Europe remains a plurality. Collaboration offers one route towards redressing that balance.

*Circumventing the imperfections of the European home market*
Everyone acknowledges that the European market, particularly for high-technology products, is awash with regulations, standards, public procurement rules, etc., which fragment the market and distort competition between firms. This fragmentation means that the right market signals are not getting through, and firms which might in other circumstances be collaborators are instead set against each other as national champion competitors. Telecommunications is perhaps a prime example here. If it were not for preferential public purchasing, national regulations and standards which divide the whole of Europe, the seven telecommunications companies currently operating in Europe might long ago have been slimmed down to two or three. Collaboration here, as in aerospace, is a 'second best' solution: it allows firms to pool research resources and share risks; and it cuts costs and enables them to remain reasonably competitive beside the majors (e.g. AT&T), while keeping market shares protected for national champions.

Why go for the 'second best' solution? Surely the best solution is to go straight for the internal market barriers themselves? If the public procurement regulations that have maintained the plethora of national champions in telecommunications were abolished, admittedly some firms would go to the wall, but would not the result be to create groupings of a size which could compete at home and perhaps globally against the AT&Ts or the IBMs of this world without having, like Airbus, to depend on the permanent crutch of national or European governmental support?

It is politics rather than economics that prevents this solution. Just as in aerospace, governments are not, when it comes to it, willing to sacrifice national champions in their high-tech industries, and therefore not really prepared to indulge in the market free-for-all this would imply. Collaboration is a useful compromise: as in aerospace, it secures some of the benefits without compromising national sovereignty, and it spreads the cost of adjustment. But as in aerospace there are costs. We cannot pretend that the lengthy and difficult negotiations necessary when four or five autonomous firms get together to develop a new product are as efficient (in terms of the use of resources) as the same procedures within a single grouping. Hence the continuing need for government involvement and often public money.

It is apparent that discussion has already moved from economics to politics. Technological collaboration may be a 'second best' to the full achievement of the internal market, but what alternative is there? Under the Treaty of Rome, the Commission has powers delegated to it in such areas as competition and the control of state aids (which are necessary for the establishment and maintenance of the common internal market and which in themselves constitute a form of 'minimalist' industry policy), but no such powers exist in relation to industrial policy proper. The Commission has to operate in this area through decisions of the Council, which have required consensus among member states, although under the Single European Act majority voting will in future be possible on some items. Not surprisingly, consensus has not been easy to achieve, which helps to explain the history of failed initiatives (discussed in Chapter 2) in establishing either a common industrial policy or a 'technology community'. It took the depth of the 1980–1 recession, the political will-power of Davignon and the threat of US deregulation to bring the Community together into the somewhat fragile consensus which established Esprit and subsequent initiatives. As the prolonged debate over the 1986 framework (R&D) budget makes clear, the consensus is indeed fragile: national sovereignty remains a potent force, and unanimity is needed for agreement on the overall package. Collaboration as a solution is, however, infinitely preferable to a situation in which each individual country subsidizes its own national champions in an attempt to enable them to compete in the global market-place.

Conclusions

The political arguments for supporting collaboration derive from the compromise it promotes between national sovereignty and full economic unity.

### Helping to achieve the internal market
Strange though it may seem, collaboration, although a compromise between maintaining national capabilities and achieving the full internal market, in fact helps to promote the achievement of the internal market. The argument runs something like this. Governments are inevitably very touchy about national sovereignty issues and overestimate their importance. As a consequence they create artificial barriers to the achievement of the internal market without fully realizing the cost (in terms of long-term competitiveness) which has to be paid. National champions not surprisingly connive with governments to keep it this way because, as they become increasingly less competitive in world markets, so the importance of protected markets increases. The advantage of collaboration is that it begins to open the eyes of national champions to what might be achieved if full use were made of a unified European market. In other words it creates a constituency, and an important constituency, which puts pressure on individual governments to back moves that help create a more unified internal market. Note, for example, the pressures coming from German industry for a relaxation of the Deutsche Bundespost monopoly in West Germany and, in particular, the pressures for full interconnection with the European telecommunications network. The pressure for the OSI standard, too, is coming from industry rather than governments. Just as the existence of a learning curve in collaboration was noted in the cases of Airbus and Esprit, so the process of working together within these programmes brings home to firms the benefits of common standards and a full common market. In this sense collaboration can be seen as a stepping-stone, but an important one, to the achievement of the full internal market.

### Helping to counter the US extraterritoriality stance
Collaboration aimed at safeguarding *European* technology may be justified as a countermeasure to the increasing technological chauvinism of our competitors, particularly the USA. The open trading system that has been built up over the postwar years has had as its adjunct open access to technology, and it is on this access that

both the West European and Japanese economies have based their success. Today that free access to US technology is being challenged. American export controls on high-technology equipment are becoming increasingly onerous for both European and US companies. Although there may well be a case for limiting exports of high-technology equipment to Eastern bloc countries, the current controls imposed on even relatively humble computer equipment pose a threat to Europe's traditionally open access to US technology. So far, the controls, while irksome, have not had a serious effect upon Europe's high-tech capabilities, or a major impact on exports to third countries. But the threat of further tightening of procedures by US authorities has led many European firms to look to European (or Japanese) sources of equipment and knowledge.[6] And there is considerable concern among British firms that the offset contracts recently agreed as part of the AWACS deal with Boeing and Westinghouse will be so loaded with extraterritoriality conditions that any potential benefits will be very limited.

It would be far better to persuade the US authorities to recognize the harm they are doing, but, given the actual and potential differences between American and European foreign policies, it is not clear that the curbs would be eased. In the circumstances, European-based technological collaboration is indeed something of an insurance policy.

*Offsetting the power of the US and Japanese multinationals*
Much of the technology transfer of the postwar years came via the US multinationals as they established subsidiaries and research centres, particularly in Europe.[7] Today, as was made clear in Chapter 1, these same multinationals are being challenged in both world and US markets by the very Japanese firms which initially, like their European counterparts, grew fat on US technology. Europe now finds itself caught as a third party in this technology war. The extraterritoriality issue itself is seen by some to represent an aspect of this war-game.[8] Equally, the tougher stance being taken by US multinationals towards their competitors, as witnessed by the very hard line IBM took on the Hitachi industrial espionage case,[9] has its spin-off effect on Europe, where US multinationals have always been viewed with slightly mixed feelings. The problem is that what is legitimate trading practice for the multinational – for

93

example, using transfer price mechanisms to help develop market shares – becomes very difficult for nationally based firms to counter.

Here indeed lies the crux of the problem. The big multinationals start with advantages in the market-place, not just in terms of the scale of production, but in terms of know-how and experience built up over time, of distribution networks, of product familiarity and – for information technology products – of software and software availability. Such advantages are well illustrated by the IBM PC, generally regarded technologically as an indifferent personal computer, which nevertheless swept the market on the basis of name, servicing, reliability and, above all, software provision. And as Sir Michael Butler pointed out, multinationals are in business to make *long-term* profit. It is not difficult to envisage a situation in which, weakened initially by the opening up of the EC internal market, the major European operators are picked off one at a time by the US and Japanese multinationals, just as the European aerospace firms might have succumbed to the major US companies had they been exposed to the full force of the market.

In this context IBM poses a problem. It is not only the major supplier of computers to European markets; it is also the major manufacturer of computers in Europe. With its extensive network of manufacturing and research facilities throughout the continent, ought it not actually to be counted as a European firm and allowed to participate in European initiatives? Indeed, partly to offset criticisms of discrimination, IBM has been allowed to take part in one (token) Esprit project; decisions on participation in Eureka projects are left to individual governments.

But there is no escaping the fact that including IBM in these initiatives is illogical. The chief aim of the collaborative programmes is to promote *European* technological competence. Making IBM or, for that matter, any US or Japanese multinational, a member of the team defeats that purpose. It channels European taxpayers' money into subsidizing, in this case, an American firm, and it effectively gives it preferential access to the research results. Discrimination there may be, but the reverse side of the coin reveals foreign companies being deliberately excluded from MITI collaborative projects in Japan and from private American initiatives such as the MCC. If we are worried about the power wielded by US and Japanese firms in world markets, and see collaborative initiatives as a way of offsetting such power, then it is not sensible to make these foreign companies members of the club.

Collaboration, once again, should be seen as an insurance policy. It helps to strengthen the technological base of European industry and thus its competitiveness, while at the same time providing an opportunity for the gradual opening up of the market to both internal and external competition.

**The costs of collaboration**

There are, however, dangers that collaboration, far from providing a constituency pressing for the abolition of internal controls, may do precisely the opposite and act instead as a mechanism for partitioning the market. The current trade-offs being suggested between the French and the Germans in the CGE/ITT and Siemens/CGTC affairs are precisely of this kind. Far from opening up the French and German markets to competition in telecommunications, it would appear that the French are offering Siemens control of CGTC as a direct trade-off for the acquisition by CGE of the SEL/ITT 12 per cent share of the West German switching market.[10]

Collaboration and cartelization are never far apart. Given the history of coordinated activity among Europe's dominant firms (it is notable, for example, that the recession of 1975–82 brought a resurgence of the chemical and man-made fibre cartels), there are obvious dangers that collaboration on so-called pre-competitive research will ultimately produce collaboration in market-sharing. This justifies the somewhat defensive stand of DG IV (the Competition Directorate) on the proclivities of DG XIII (responsible for IT and telecommunications) towards collaborative ventures. If there are benefits to be gained from collaboration, it is important that they are reaped by the Community as a whole and not transformed into monopoly or oligopoly profits and special pleading for protection from the full rigours of the market.

Allied to the collaboration/cartelization issue is that of what constitutes pre-competitive research. It has long been accepted that governments have a role in promoting and paying for basic scientific research, because by its nature it does not produce anything that can be appropriated, and there is therefore no incentive for private enterprise to fund it. Likewise, it is also accepted that whenever the application of scientific research leads to commercially useful results, it is both apt and right that private enterprise foot the bill. In the middle, however, is the grey area labelled pre-competitive research: research that is targeted at a specific problem, yet whose results in themselves do not lead directly to commercial products. This is not a distinction that can always be maintained. Pre-competitive programmes, if successful, lead to appropriable developments in techniques and products. Indeed, as with both the Alvey and Esprit programmes, it is at the second stage of funding that the distinction becomes especially difficult to maintain: there are obvious pressures from those engaged in the initial research to be allowed to exploit it subsequently. Coordination of research effort thus spills over into coordination of market shares.

All this points in two directions. First, there is a need for a strong and coherent competition policy, capable of resisting tendencies to cartelization and the abuse of market power. DG IV could do worse than model itself on the US anti-trust laws, whose vigilant application, as Chapter 1 described, has done much to limit the power of the giant firm in the USA. Europe badly needs to find ways of encouraging some of its minnows to grow into big fish.

The completion of the internal market both helps and hinders the role of DG IV. On the one hand it makes its role more straightforward – no longer will it be constrained by the myriad of national regulations which currently cut into its effectiveness. But on the other, it adds to its load since, logically, there will be no need for each member state to maintain an independent anti-trust authority once the internal market has been achieved. Indeed, there is much to be said for DG IV building up its role in the course of the next few years in anticipation of this development. It is also important that competition authorities, perhaps working in conjunction with the GATT and OECD, increase their clout with multinational companies. At present it is all too easy for multinationals to gain market share by switching resources around from country to country via transfer pricing and similar techniques. Trade and competition policy need to go hand in hand.

Second, there is a need to decide on the direction of the collaborative programme. In a recent paper,[11] Henry Ergas drew a distinction between the 'mission-oriented' R&D policies of the USA, France and Britain, in which developments in new technologies are spearheaded by targeted policies, frequently linked to defence needs and capabilities; and the 'diffusion-oriented' approaches of West Germany and Scandinavia, in which the emphasis is on the broad diffusion of new techniques into the existing industrial base. (Japan, as he points out, falls between the two.) Of the mission-oriented countries he finds the USA the most successful, largely because it has effective mechanisms for diffusing its highly targeted strategies into the industrial fabric of society. France is considerably less successful in doing this, and the UK even worse. But from a European point of view, what is interesting is the success which he attributes to the West German and Scandinavian diffusion-oriented systems. These are built upon a broad base of skilled labour and on policies aimed not at promoting one or two mainstream areas of technology, but at encouraging the updating of equipment and technique across the board.

To date, the European programmes have been somewhat hybrid. Brite and Comett are clearly diffusion-based, as is Eureka, which now has a distinct 'bottom up' orientation. Esprit tends more towards the mission-oriented, but, given its diversity and its emphasis on bringing new developments into use, retains a strong practical bent. The one programme that is most obviously mission-oriented is Race, in telecommunications. Yet, considering its aim is to provide the basic infrastructure for the development of the 'information society' of the next century, it is a moot point whether Europe can really afford to drop it in the hope that the market will pick it up of its own volition. Given the considerable externalities involved in the development of a broadband communications network, there is reason to doubt whether a full network which yields maximum benefit to all would be provided by anything but a public authority.

In narrow economic terms there is only a weak case for European governments actively promoting collaboration between European firms. There are benefits to be derived from a wider exchange of information and from the higher level of R&D expenditures which public investment programmes probably stimulate. But there are also costs: there is the deadweight cost of subsidizing expenditure which would have been undertaken anyway, and there is the additional risk of creating circumstances in which price agreements and market sharing can more easily take place.

Strategic and political factors swing the balance in favour of collaboration. If the world operated according to benign free-trade rules, then it would be a matter of indifference whether partners were European, American or Japanese. But the world does not operate in this way. Global competition is tough and relentless. Given the current performance of US and Japanese multinationals and the trading policies pursued by their governments, it is impossible to be confident that what seem benign trading partnerships of today will not lead to technological dependency tomorrow.

Collaboration offers a constructive alternative to protection. It is vital to improve the competitiveness of European firms, especially in IT. This can partly be effected by the completion of the internal market, but that in turn will expose firms to considerable competitive strain. An incentive to look towards European partners at this juncture will help to prevent what might be described as a 'weakness take-out', namely, selling out to the USA or Japan. A collaborative programme with public subsidy to help cement European partnerships may help promote rapid adjustment and facilitate progress towards the internal market.

Nevertheless, collaboration carries costs, and it is vital that they be minimized. This can best be achieved by, first, unremitting pressure to see the achievement of the full internal market, to which collaboration is not an *alternative*; second, a more rigorous competition policy within the EC, to avoid cartelization or the abuse of the market; and, third, continued emphasis on the use and diffusion of new technologies, while eschewing the temptation to turn national champions into European champions.

**Britain's position**
What view should the UK take of European technological collaboration? Do its interests coincide with those of the rest of Europe, or are they in any way different? As Chapter 1 made clear, while Europe as a whole has no reason to worry overmuch about any technology gap, the UK's position is considerably less satisfactory than that of most of its European competitors. In shares of patents, industrially funded R&D, scientific publications – indeed any index of technological performance – Britain's record is generally worse than that of any major European country. There are only two high-technology industries – pharmaceuticals and aerospace – in which the UK's sectoral record is in any sense distinguished. It has abjectly failed to do what the West Germans have achieved in machine tools,

namely turn the tide on the Japanese; indeed, British firms in this sector have all but disappeared except in tiny niche markets, thereby epitomizing the problems of British industry. In spite of early access to US technology in numerically controlled (NC) and computer numerically controlled (CNC) machine tools, the UK industry failed until too late to recognize the need to bring electronics into the product range, and as a consequence it found its market at home and abroad swept from under it, first by US firms, then by the Japanese, and now by German and Swiss manufacturers. The British industry today is dominated by US and Japanese subsidiaries; British firms contribute only a fraction of the total output, and most of the substantive R&D is done outside the UK.[12]

Can technological collaboration help Britian overcome this crisis of competitiveness? The answer is: 'Yes, to a limited degree.' But collaboration is not and cannot be a panacea for all the UK's ills. Collaboration can, as for other European countries, offer a route for the spreading of costs and risks; it can provide technological know-how and complementary assets; and it also helps to focus the attention of British firms on the global rather than the UK market. But, as the machine tool case illustrates so well, where there is collaboration, each side needs to have something to give. If the UK has no technological advantage to trade, then the price of buying in technology may be the sacrifice of substantial market share.

The UK remains an amazingly creative society, but its technological heritage is now sadly depleted. As the Nimrod episode illustrates so aptly, even in the one area of electronics where most government resources have been put, namely defence electronics, the UK has had difficulty in producing a competitive product. Just as with inward investment, technological collaboration can bring new know-how and new products and widen horizons to embrace new management styles, all of which are valuable contributions to improving British industrial performance. But it may also expose the British economy to the predatory capture of market share by foreign multinationals, which is difficult to control once the door has been opened. The danger is that there will be too many industries like machine tools, in which the price for technological know-how is the surrendering of a substantial part of the market share, and in which British manufacturers retreat to an ever smaller corner.

In this respect, technological collaboration for the UK becomes something of a Hobson's choice. To eschew such deals is foolish in a world where competition is increasingly globalized, for all the reasons which have been reiterated in this paper. Equally, given the UK's relative competitive and technological weakness within the world economy, its bargaining power is limited and there are dangers of technological dependency if its chosen partners are always American or Japanese. Witness what has happened in some regions of the UK already, where the 'branch economy' syndrome has brought assembly plants, but a singular lack of R&D establishments or even European headquarters. In these circumstances, collaboration within Europe offers a half-way house. It has a number of distinct advantages. It provides an element of protection, yet may also confront the firm with more competition than hitherto, as national markets are opened up to Europe. In this sense it may be a useful way of weaning firms used to privileged access to national markets and forcing them to face the realities of global competition. Nor does it exclude the possibility of American and Japanese partnerships if these seem appropriate. As we saw in Chapter 4, many firms combine participation in one or more of the European programmes with more specific links outside the Community. But it does enable the firm, should it need to, to draw upon the collective weight of the EC to counter the economic power of the USA and Japan.

In the long run, if the UK wishes to remain one of Europe's major industrial powers, a solution must be sought not just through collaboration, but through domestic economic and industrial policies. Britain has to put its own house in order and strengthen its industrial base. Prime consideration needs to be given to education and training, the promotion of industrial R&D, and the development of long-term strategic thinking. Programmes under way in Europe can help in all these areas.

In this context it is worth remarking upon the short-sightedness of the Treasury-inspired guidelines for public expenditure, which require spending departments to include allocations for EC programmes within their existing expenditure ceilings. In practice this means that the opportunity cost of participating in EC programmes of collaborative R&D may well be the loss of equivalent expenditures for national programmes – e.g., more for UK biotechnology from the EC means less from the Department of Trade and Industry. Thus, while involvement in EC programmes may shift the emphasis towards transnational collaboration, it does not increase total **R&D** expenditure in the UK. Given the cash limits, it is not surprising officials are often lukewarm in their promotion of EC programmes: they are obviously anxious to see their own programmes flourish.

Overall, therefore, British firms stand to benefit from technological collaboration, and European partnerships may have more to offer than is currently apparent. However, there are long-term costs in technological dependency, as illustrated by the 'branch economy' syndrome in some UK regions and in Ireland. But the need for British firms to look outwards, beyond the confines of the British market, suggests that there is an advantage in backing initiatives which provide an incentive for firms to 'think European'. What is clear, though, is that the benefits from collaboration, whether with European or non-European firms, will only come if Britain simultaneously strengthens its economic and industrial base. Collaboration may help, but it should not obscure the need for these changes in domestic policy.

## Summing up and recommendations

Economic and commercial criteria provide only a limited case for promoting technological collaboration within Europe, with the elements of subsidy and protection that accompany it. Political and strategic factors, however, provide much stronger arguments. The case against the free-market solution, in which internal and external protective barriers are simultaneously removed, is not only that of practical implementation – one has only to observe the contortions of free-market West Germany when faced by the innate protectionism of the Deutsche Bundespost to realize how difficult it is going to be to achieve the internal market objectives by the early 1990s – but also that, quite frankly, in some important high-technology areas European firms could not face the competition. The danger is then that, given this weakness, American and Japanese companies would fall upon the market and divide it among themselves.

Perhaps this does not matter. It is a moot point whether technological dependence is necessarily a 'bad thing', but those who point to the benign world of the 1950s should bear in mind that the game has shifted. The USA now jealously guards its technology, as the endless extraterritoriality issues over COCOM controls indicate only too readily. In this, the European countries may be unwitting third parties to the technology war between the USA and Japan; but the knock-on effects certainly mean that the days of open access to US technology are gone.

Collaboration in this respect should be seen as a second best option. It is on the agenda because governments wish to retain an independent presence, at either a national or a European level, in a particular sector or industry. As a second best option, it has certain advantages. It is a method of strengthening the competitive edge of at least some European firms, while allowing for a progressive diminution of protection over time. It helps to boost spending on R&D – and one of Europe's failings is the reluctance of its firms to spend on R&D – and last, but by no means least, it creates a constituency which has experienced the benefits of working, and thinking, at a European level and which recognizes the benefits to be obtained from the completion of the internal market. For too long it has been just the economists, and not the industrialists, who have been talking of the advantages of unified markets.

Such a policy is in no sense anti-American or anti-Japanese. These countries themselves operate within the international community as nation states, promoting and pursuing their own national interests by means of a judicious mixture of subsidy and protection. The market forces which European firms encounter in global competition are themselves partly shaped by the political interventions of the US and Japanese governments.

Europe at present tends to fall between two stools in establishing where its industrial and technological interests lie. Commercial policy decisions, for which the Treaty of Rome gives clear responsibility to the EC, are now taken at a Community level, where the Commission negotiates collectively (to considerable effect). But this is not true of industrial policy, for which the EC does not operate as a single entity, although logic argues that it should do so with the completion of the internal market. As the relative importance of the nation state within the European context declines, it will become more important that there are effective institutions within the EC to uphold the interests of European firms *vis-à-vis* their stronger brethren from Japan and the USA. If these two countries can act on occasion in support of narrow self-interest, so too should Europe. One advantage of 'contrived collaboration' is that it offers an element of protection which would be available to be traded away against tangible concessions.

There are of course dangers as well as advantages in promoting technological collaboration, not least the continuing suspicion that it will merely translate national into European champions, and that, as with the Common Agricultural Policy, we shall end up by having to maintain uneconomic and unnecessary capacity. There is also the danger of subsidizing firms in R&D that they would have to do anyway, and the constant risk of collusion. But the worst of these disadvantages can be overcome by gearing the programme to collaborative initiatives which, like Brite and Eureka, encourage the small and medium-sized firm; making sure that the smaller firm gets an entrée into major programmes such as Esprit; using a mechanism such as the EUROTYPE badge proposed under Eureka to give preference in public purchasing to some of the smaller European firms; promoting programmes, such as Comett, which aim to improve the technological infrastructure, particularly, as in this case, the education and training infrastructure; promoting the private venture capital market (as does Eureka); and so on. Perhaps the most important action should be taken in strengthening competition policy, in which Community-level initiatives become the more necessary as the completion of the internal market puts increasing pressure on Community institutions, and the scope of which logically includes the multinationals operating within the Community as much as European firms themselves.

The prescription therefore runs as follows:

1. Do not regard collaboration as a panacea for all of Europe's, let alone the UK's, high-technology problems, but support it, and support it whole-heartedly. Decisions about European initiatives for R&D should be taken on their own merit and not be subordinated to the long-running problems of agricultural expenditure, nor in the UK to the short-sighted insistence on domestic cash ceilings.

2. Do not let the Community, or Europe, cut itself off from the rest of the world, but, equally, let it be just as ready as the USA or Japan to act on occasion in a self-interested manner. This implies that collaboration should not be exclusively with European firms, but equally that the EC should be prepared to discriminate against non-European multinationals within its collaborative programmes, just as the USA and Japan discriminate against foreign firms.

3. Reinforce strongly the measures taken to secure the completion of the internal market, including those involving public pro-

curement, and work for the rapid achievement of unified standards and regulations in the high-technology sectors.

4. Combine these measures with a tough anti-trust stance which involves both a hawklike watch on tendencies towards cartelization and surveillance of abuse of dominant position by indigenous and multinational firms alike.

5. Find some means whereby some of Europe's minnows grow into bigger fish. This may involve both the opening up of capital markets, which currently favour the large firm, and some degree of positive discrimination by ensuring, for example, that a certain proportion of public contracts go to smaller firms. Such positive discrimination needs to be carried over also into collaborative programmes such as Esprit, in order to ensure that there is a continuing technological challenge to the complacency of large firms.

6. Finally and most importantly, within the broader national and European framework, adopt policies which are complementary to these collaborative programmes and which promote flexibility in the European economies. First and foremost among these should be policies designed to improve the skills and adaptability of the workforce.

# STATISTICAL
# APPENDIX TO
# CHAPTER 1

Table 1.1 Minimum investment required for memory chip
production

| Year | RAM vintage | $m required for wafer fabrication plant | Time required for development |
|------|-------------|------------------------------------------|-------------------------------|
| 1966 | 16-bit | 0.5 | 6 months |
| 1970 | 250-bit | 1.0 | — |
| 1974 | 1K | 2.0 | 1 year |
| 1978 | 4K | 5.0 | — |
| 1980 | 16K | 10.0 | 2 years |
| 1984 | 256K | 50.0 | — |
| 1986 | 1M | 100.0 | 3 years |
| 1987 | 4M | 200.0 | — |

*Sources*: OECD, *The Semiconductor Industry: Trade Related Issues* (Paris, OECD, 1985) and Erik Arnold and Ken Guy, *Parallel Convergence* (London, Frances Pinter, 1986).

Table 1.2 **R&D** as a proportion of economic resources

|  |  | Japan | USA | W. Europe |
|---|---|---|---|---|
| Total **R&D** as | 1967 | 1.58 | 3.07 | 1.78 |
| % of GDP | 1975 | 2.01 | 2.38 | 1.81 |
|  | 1983 | 2.67 | 2.73 | 2.08 |
| Civil **R&D** as | 1967 | 1.56 | 1.97 | 1.47 |
| % of GDP | 1975 | 2.00 | 1.75 | 1.57 |
|  | 1983 | 2.66 | 1.97 | 1.80 |
| Industrial **R&D** | 1967 | 0.92 | 2.35 | 1.27 |
| as % of industrial | 1975 | 1.28 | 1.84 | 1.35 |
| value added* | 1983 | 2.16 | 2.20 | 1.67 |
| Industry-financed | 1967 | 0.90 | 1.15 | 0.92 |
| R&D as % of indus- | 1975 | 1.26 | 1.18 | 1.00 |
| trial value added | 1983 | 2.12 | 1.50 | 1.28 |

*Industry includes agriculture, mining, construction and the utilities as well as manufacturing.
*Source*: OECD, via Pari Patel and Keith Pavitt, 'Is Europe losing the technology race?', *Research Policy*, no. 1 (1987).

Table 1.3 Growth rates of industrially funded R&D

| Country | 1967–83 | 1967–75 | 1975–83 |
|---|---|---|---|
| Japan | 10.8 | 10.6 | 10.9 |
| USA | 4.1 | 2.4 | 5.7 |
| W. Europe | 4.4 | 4.3 | 4.5 |

*Source*: OECD, quoted in Pari Patel and Keith Pavitt, 'Is Europe losing the technology race?', *Research Policy,* no. 1 (1987).

Table 1.4 Intra-European variations in industry-financed R&D in 1983

| Country | Percentage share of European total | Proportion of value added (%) | $ per capita | % growth p.a. 1967–83 | Defence as a % of GERD |
|---------|------------|------------|------------|------------|------------|
| W. Germany | 35.6 | 1.86 | 96.4 | 5.64 | 4.3 |
| France | 18.7 | 1.15 | 57.7 | 5.80 | 21.4 |
| UK | 16.6 | 1.22 | 49.5 | 1.08 | 29.2 |
| Italy | 8.5 | 0.60 | 25.0 | 5.12 | 3.4 |
| Switzerland | 5.3 | n.a. | 136.8 | 1.80 | 1.5 |
| Sweden | 5.5 | 2.18 | 109.4 | 6.59 | 10.7 |
| Netherlands | 4.7 | 1.18 | 54.9 | 2.01 | 1.5 |
| Belgium | 3.8 | 1.33 | 64.9 | 6.53 | (*) |
| Denmark | 1.1 | 0.82 | 35.4 | 5.34 | (*) |
| Ireland | 0.3 | 0.51 | 13.6 | 7.45 | (*) |

GERD = Gross expenditure on R&D.
*In Belgium, Denmark and Ireland, defence R&D accounted for less than 1% of GERD.
*Source*: Pari Patel and Keith Pavitt, 'Is Europe losing the technology race?', *Research Policy*, no. 1 (1987).

Table 1.5 Shares of US patenting by West European countries (%)

| Country | 1963 | 1969 | 1976 | 1985 |
|---------|------|------|------|------|
| W. Germany | 33.9 | 35.9 | 38.4 | 42.2 |
| UK | 26.3 | 25.0 | 18.6 | 15.8 |
| France | 12.4 | 14.2 | 15.0 | 15.2 |
| Switzerland | 9.7 | 8.3 | 9.2 | 7.8 |
| Sweden | 5.6 | 5.3 | 6.2 | 5.4 |
| Netherlands | 4.8 | 4.4 | 4.6 | 4.8 |
| Italy | 5.0 | 4.4 | 5.2 | 5.8 |
| Belgium | 1.2 | 1.7 | 1.8 | 1.5 |
| Denmark | 1.0 | 1.1 | 1.1 | 1.1 |
| Ireland | 0.0 | 0.1 | 0.1 | 0.2 |
|  | 100.0 | 100.0 | 100.0 | 100.0 |

*Source*: Office of Technology Assessment and Forecasts, US Patent and Trade Mark Office, Washington, D.C.

Table 1.6 Sectoral distribution of total industrial R&D in 1981 (%)

| Country | Total | Chemicals | Machinery | Metals | Transport | Aerospace |
|---|---|---|---|---|---|---|
| Japan | 16.1 | 17.7 | 15.6 | 32.7 | 24.7 | 0 |
| USA | 53.6 | 45.2 | 55.4 | 38.6 | 45.9 | 77.3 |
| W. Europe* | 30.3 | 37.1 | 29.0 | 28.7 | 29.9 | 22.7 |
| Total | 100.0 | 100.0 | 100.0 | 100.0 | 100.0 | 100.0 |

*Excluding the Netherlands and Switzerland.
*Source*: Pari Patel and Keith Pavitt, 'Is Europe losing the technology race?', *Research Policy*, no. 1 (1987), derived from OECD data.

Table 1.7 Patterns and trends of technological advantage in Western Europe

| Increasing | Stable | Decreasing |
|---|---|---|
| *Advantage* | | |
| Agricultural chemicals | Drugs and medicines | Industrial organic chemistry |
| Soaps and detergents | Primary ferrous products | Industrial inorganic chemistry |
| Metal-working machinery | Special industrial machinery | Plastics and synthetic resins |
| Household appliances | General industrial machinery | Primary and secondary non-ferrous products |
| Miscellaneous electrical machinery | Miscellaneous non-electrical machinery | Engines and turbines |
| Nuclear reactors and systems | Electrical industrial apparatus | Motor vehicles |
| Aircraft and parts | | |
| *Disadvantage* | | |
| Food | Paints and varnishes | Office computing |
| Miscellaneous chemical products | Petroleum and gas | Radio and TV |

Table 1.7 concluded

| Increasing | Stable | Decreasing |
|---|---|---|
| *Disadvantage* (*concl.*) | | |
| Fabricated metal | Rubber and plastics | Electronic components; telecommunications equipment |
| Farm and garden machinery | Electrical transmission | Instruments |
| Construction and mining equipment | Guided missiles and space vehicles | |
| Refrigeration equipment | | |
| Electric lighting and wiring | | |

*Note*: The concept of 'technological advantage' is analogous to the concept of comparative advantage in trade. Using patent data (registrations for US patents) one can identify sectors in which patent share is increasing or decreasing in comparison to the average. This table looks at Europe's shares of patents in different sectors and categorizes them according to whether that share as a whole is above average (i.e., advantage or disadvantage), and shows whether Europe is increasing or decreasing its relative share.

*Source*: Pari Patel and Keith Pavitt, 'Is Europe losing the technology race?', *Research Policy*, no. 1 (1987).

Table 1.8 Percentage shares of world exports in technology-intensive products

| Country | 1965 | 1970 | 1975 | 1980 | 1981 | 1982 | 1983 | 1984 |
|---|---|---|---|---|---|---|---|---|
| USA | 27.5 | 27.0 | 24.5 | 22.9 | 23.0 | 24.7 | 25.1 | 25.2 |
| Japan | 7.3 | 10.9 | 11.6 | 14.3 | 17.4 | 16.2 | 17.8 | 20.2 |
| France | 7.3 | 7.1 | 8.4 | 8.5 | 7.9 | 8.3 | 7.7 | 7.7 |
| W. Germany | 16.9 | 16.8 | 16.8 | 16.3 | 14.8 | 15.5 | 15.0 | 14.5 |
| UK | 12.0 | 9.8 | 9.6 | 10.8 | 9.0 | 9.4 | 8.7 | 8.5 |

*Note*: Reflects information from 24 reporting countries on exports to, and imports from, each of nearly 200 partner countries.

Technology-intensive products are defined as those for which R&D expenditures exceed 2.36 per cent of value added (OECD definition).

*Source*: DRI Special Tabulations of International Trade (Washington, D.C., National Science Foundation, 1986).

Table 1.9 World export shares of technology-intensive products, 1984 (%)

| Product field | USA | Japan | W. Germany (1) | France (2) | UK (3) | (1)+(2)+(3) |
|---|---|---|---|---|---|---|
| Aircraft and parts | 45.1 | 0.5 | 15.2 | 11.8 | 14.5 | 41.5 |
| Industrial inorganic chemicals | 23.9 | 4.3 | 15.0 | 11.5 | 12.2 | 38.7 |
| Radio and TV receiving equipment | 0.5 | 79.5 | 8.2 | 1.0 | 2.2 | 11.4 |
| Office and computing machines | 35.5 | 19.1 | 9.2 | 5.6 | 9.5 | 24.3 |
| Electrical machinery and equipment | 23.9 | 19.3 | 17.3 | 8.2 | 9.2 | 35.1 |
| Communications equipment | 26.5 | 35.5 | 10.4 | 6.1 | 6.4 | 22.9 |
| Professional and scientific instruments | 13.7 | 31.2 | 15.3 | 5.7 | 7.4 | 28.4 |
| Drugs | 19.6 | 2.6 | 15.8 | 10.7 | 11.9 | 37.8 |
| Plastic materials, synthetics | 14.4 | 10.1 | 21.4 | 9.5 | 6.9 | 37.8 |
| Engines and turbines | 29.9 | 17.4 | 16.4 | 1.9 | 8.7 | 27.0 |
| Agriculture | 33.7 | 4.1 | 13.9 | 7.2 | 7.2 | 27.4 |

*Note:* Reflects information from 24 reporting countries on exports to, and imports from, each of nearly 200 partner countries. Technology-intensive products are defined as those for which R&D expenditures exceed 2.36 per cent of value added. (OECD definition).
*Source:* DRI Special Tabulations of International Trade (Washington, D.C., National Science Foundation, 1986).

Table 1.10 Comparisons of the commercialization and diffusion of significant innovations

| Sector | Measure | Relative ranking of three regions | | | Within Europe | |
|--------|---------|-------|-----|-----------|--------|------|
| | | Japan | USA | W. Europe | Strong | Weak |
| Pharma-ceuticals | Per capita production of 'new chemical entities', 1961–83 | 2= | 2= | 1 | (*) | (*) |
| Basic steel-making | Proportion of steel-making in 1970s using oxygen or electric technique | 1 | 3 | 2 | Austria W. Germany Italy Sweden | France UK |
| Continuous casting | Proportion of steel-making using continuous casting, 1975–81 | 1 | 3 | 2 | France W. Germany Italy Sweden | Belgium UK |
| Numerically controlled machine tools | Per capita production of numerically controlled machine tools, 1979 | 1 | 2= | 2= | W. Germany Italy | France UK |
| Robots | Robots per 1000 manufacturing employees in 1983 | 1 | 3 | 2 | W. Germany Sweden | France UK |
| Integrated circuits | Per capita use of integrated circuits in 1982 | 2 | 1 | 3 | (*) | (*) |
| Software | Sales of traded software in 1982 in USA, France and Japan | 3 | 1 | 2 | (*) | (*) |

*Data not available.
*Source*: Pari Patel and Keith Pavitt, 'Is Europe losing the technology race?', *Research Policy*, no. 1 (1987).

Table 1.11 Distribution of scientific publications (%)

| Country | 1973 | 1974 | 1975 | 1976 | 1977 | 1978 | 1979 | 1980 | 1981 | 1982 |
|---------|------|------|------|------|------|------|------|------|------|------|
| Japan | 7.1 | 7.0 | 7.3 | 7.7 | 8.1 | 8.7 | 8.8 | 9.5 | 9.8 | 10.1 |
| USA | 54.4 | 53.5 | 52.7 | 52.8 | 52.4 | 51.8 | 52.0 | 51.0 | 51.1 | 51.1 |
| W. Europe | 38.5 | 39.5 | 40.0 | 39.5 | 39.5 | 39.5 | 39.2 | 39.5 | 39.1 | 38.8 |
| Total | 100 | 100 | 100 | 100 | 100 | 100 | 100 | 100 | 100 | 100 |

*Source*: CHI/NFF, Science Literature Indicators Data Base, Washington, D.C.

Table 1.12 Indices of revealed scientific advantage in 1982

| Discipline | Japan | USA | W. Europe |
|------------|-------|-----|-----------|
| Clinical medicine | 0.768 | 1.140 | 1.153 |
| Biomedical research | 0.887 | 1.111 | 1.006 |
| Biology | 0.905 | 1.191 | 0.751 |
| Chemistry | 1.577 | 0.592 | 0.962 |
| Physics | 1.225 | 0.801 | 0.970 |
| Earth and space science | 0.287 | 1.165 | 0.849 |
| Engineering and technology | 1.071 | 1.124 | 0.897 |
| Mathematics | 0.820 | 1.046 | 1.002 |

*Note*: A figure greater than 1 indicates a relative gain; less than 1 indicates a relative loss.
*Source*: CHI/NFF, Science Literature Indicators Data Base, Washington, D.C..

Table 1.13 Inter-firm agreements in the electronics industry

| Area | Before 1982 (total) | 1982 | 1983 | 1984 |
|------|------|------|------|------|
| W. Europe/W. Europe | 22 | 7 | 23 | 33 |
| USA/USA | 13 | 6 | 20 | 28 |
| W. Europe/USA | 61 | 34 | 36 | 43 |
| Japan/USA | 18 | 10 | 19 | 9 |
| Japan/W. Europe | 17 | 12 | 5 | 5 |
| Total | 131 | 69 | 104 | 118 |

*Note*: Based on newspaper and trade press reports collated by Reseau (Milan).
*Source*: OECD Secretariat, *Technical Cooperation Agreements between Firms: Some Initial Data and Analysis*, DSTI/SPR/86.20., Pt I (Paris, OECD, 1986).

Table 1.14 A sample of agreements involving European firms by year of establishment and main objective.

| Year | Knowledge | Production | Marketing | Global | Total |
|------|-----------|------------|-----------|--------|-------|
| 1980 | 11 | 12 | 6 | 2 | 15 |
| 1981 | 15 | 13 | 10 | 10 | 31 |
| 1982 | 17 | 16 | 15 | 24 | 58 |
| 1983 | 24 | 25 | 31 | 41 | 97 |
| 1984 | 36 | 37 | 36 | 57 | 131 |
| 1985 | 47 | 39 | 51 | 58 | 149 |
| Total | 150 | 142 | 149 | 192 | 481 |

*Note*: derived from reports in French press collated by LAREA/CEREM Datis.
*Source*: OECD Secretariat, *Technical Cooperation Agreements between Firms: Some Initial Data and Analysis*, DSTI/SPR/86.20., Pt I (Paris, OECD, 1986).

# NOTES

*Chapter 1*

1 OECD Secretariat, *Technical Cooperation Agreements between Firms: Some Initial Data and Analysis*, DSTI/SPR/86.20, Part I (Paris, OECD, 1986), p. 3.

2 The block exemption is limited. It only applies to collaborators in so far as they do not jointly hold more than 20 per cent of the market for the products resulting from the collaboration, or of the market for the products improved or replaced by that collaboration in the EC or a substantial part of it; and joint exploitation is taken to include production or licensing of the intellectual property rights or know-how generated by the project, but not distribution or marketing. Collaboration at the final marketing stage remains the subject of tight scrutiny on a case-by-case basis.

3 David Landes, *The Unbound Prometheus* (Cambridge, Cambridge University Press, 1969).

4 Ed Sciberras, in his book *Multinational Electronics Companies and National Economic Policies: A Study of Competitive Behaviour* (Greenwich, CT, Jai Press, 1977), noted the tendency for the semi-conductor industry to divide itself into 'big league' and 'little league' players, and he emphasized the difficulty for the little league players of achieving dynamic economies of scale. However, Japanese electronics multinationals were able to enter these markets from a position of relative (technological) weakness.

5  See Pari Patel and Keith Pavitt, 'Is Europe losing the technological race?', *Research Policy*, no. 1 (1987).

6  John Irvine and Ben Martin, *Foresight in Science* (London, Frances Pinter, 1985).

7  The concept of the technology gap first emerged in the 1950s, when econmists pinpointed increases in knowledge as the main factor explaining variations in growth. The fast growth of West Germany, France, Italy and Japan was largely explained by their ability to gain rapid access to US technology. The slowing down of European growth rates in the 1970s was at first explained by the fact that Europe had 'caught up' with the USA. It could, however, be argued that on both occasions the gap was more of a managerial phenomenon than a question of access to technology.

8  Erik Arnold, in his study of the European computer-aided design industry – *Computer Aided Design*, Sussex European Paper no. 14 (Science Policy Research Unit, University of Sussex, 1984) – also argues that once the US firms had established their foothold in the European market in the late 1970s, it was difficult for others to break in, although in the late 1960s European firms had failed to capitalize on the advantage they had at that time.

9  This is chronicled in J. Horn, H. Klodt and C. Saunders, 'Advanced Machine Tools: Production Diffusion and Trade', in Margaret Sharp, ed., *Europe and the New Technologies* (London, Frances Pinter, 1985).

10  Ibid.

11  See Alan Cane's article, 'Now Europe may be ready to strike back', in *The Financial Times*, 15 July 1986.

12  Under the anti-trust settlement with AT&T in 1956, it was agreed that the company would not manufacture semiconductors for the open market (i.e., only for its own use), and that its patents on transistors and semiconductors would effectively be put into the public domain – that is, available for use by all comers free of charge. In addition, Bell labs provided 'training' in their technology and use for any who wished to avail themselves of the facilities. This important development provided the break from which many of the new US semiconductor firms took root and grew. See Stanford Research Institute, 'Strategic Partnerships: A New Corporate Response' (Stanford, CA, SRI International Associates Programme, Report no. 730, 1986).

13  See Erik Arnold and Ken Guy, *Parellel Convergence* (London, Frances Pinter, 1986).

14  Ronald Dore, *A Case Study of Technological Forecasting in Japan: The Next Generation Base Technologies Development Programme* (London, Technical Change Centre, 1983).

15 See Godefroy Dang Nguyen, 'Telecommunications: A Challenge to the Old Order', in Sharp, ed., *Europe and the New Technologies*, pp. 102–4.

16 Ibid., p. 108.

17 See Michael McClean, *The Inmos Saga* (London, Frances Pinter, 1984).

18 Sharp, ed., *Europe and the New Technologies*, p. 103.

19 See M. Kaldor, M. Sharp and W. Walker, 'Industrial competitiveness and Britain's defence', *Lloyds Bank Review*, October 1986.

20 For a discussion of the concept of the *filière*, see Godefroy Dang Nguyen and Erik Arnold, 'Videotex: Much Ado About Nothing?', in Sharp, ed., *Europe and the New Technologies*, pp. 135–8.

21 For a brief but authoritative account of recent French economic/industrial policy, see Peter Holmes and Anne Stevens, *The Framework of Government: Industry Relations and Industrial Policy-making in France*, Working Paper on Government-Industry Relations no. 2 (University of Sussex, June 1986).

22 Stanford Research Institute, 'Strategic Partnerships' (footnote 12).

23 D.J. Teece, 'Capturing Value from Technological Integration: Strategic Partnering and Licensing Decisions', paper prepared for the Venice Conference on Innovation Diffusion, Department of Economics, Venice University, 1986.

24 K. Ohmae, *Triad Power: The Coming Shape of Global Competition* (London and Basingstoke, Collier Macmillan, 1985), p. 173.

*Chapter 2*

1 F.G. Clark and Arthur Gibson, *Concorde: The Story of the World's Most Advanced Passenger Aircraft* (London, Phoebus Publishing, 1976), p. 2. Two other books on Concorde worth looking at are G. Knight, *Concorde: The Inside Story* (London, Weidenfeld & Nicolson, 1976), and E.J. Feldman, *Concorde and Dissent: Explaining High Technology Failures in Britain and France* (Cambridge, Cambridge University Press, 1985).

2 Jean-Jacques Servan-Schreiber, *Le Défi Américain* (Paris, Denoël, 1967).

3 *Opinion on the Applications for Membership Received from the UK, Ireland, Denmark and Norway* (Brussels, Commission of the European Communities, 1967).

4 *Scientific and Technological Aspects of the Extension of the European Communities*, Doc. 2279 (Strasbourg, Council of Europe, 1967), p. 30.

5 Harold Wilson, *The Labour Government 1964–70* (London, Weidenfeld & Nicolson and Michael Joseph, 1971), p. 300, referred to in

Roger Williams, *European Technology: The Politics of Collaboration* (London, Croom Helm, 1973), pp. 21–2.

6 The Action Committee for the United States of Europe was founded in October 1955, on the initiative of Jean Monnet, by the Socialist, Christian Democrat and Liberal Parties, and non-Communist trade unions of six EC countries: Belgium, France, West Germany, Italy, Luxembourg and the Netherlands.

7 Christopher Layton, *European Advanced Technology: A Programme for Integration* (London, Allen & Unwin, 1969).

8 Commission Memorandum to the Council on the Establishment of European Companies, Supplement to the *Bulletin of the European Communities*, no. 9/10 (1966).

9 Commission Memorandum to the Council, 'La Politique Industrielle de la Communauté, COM (70) 100 final (Brussels, Commission of the European Communities, 1970).

10 Roger Williams, *European Technology: The Politics of Collaboration* (London, Croom Helm, 1973), p. 39.

11 For the sake of consistency, and because it is their popular name, we refer to 'fast breeder' reactors throughout, although they are also known as 'fast' reactors.

12 For further details, see Claire Shearman, 'Cooperation in fast reactors – lessons from the European experience', *Physics in Technology*, vol. 17 (1986), no. 1.

13 This provided for the pooling of system know-how within the collaboration framework. Two joint companies were set up, which then entrusted the transfer of fast breeder reactor know-how to third parties to the especially created subsidiary Serena. The term Serena is also used to refer to the whole network of agreements negotiated at this time between France (with Italy) and Germany (for the Debene countries).

14 For further details, see Keith Hayward, *International Collaboration in Civil Aerospace* (London, Frances Pinter, 1986). His other useful book on aerospace is *Government and British Civil Aerospace* (Manchester, Manchester University Press, 1983). We are most grateful to Keith Hayward for his help and advice on this section.

15 Hayward, *International Collaboration in Civil Aerospace*, p. 55.

16 Ibid., p. 63.

17 Christopher Layton, 'The High-Tech Triangle', in Roger Morgan and Caroline Bray (eds), *Partners and Rivals in Western Europe: Britain, France and Germany* (Aldershot, Gower for the Policy Studies Institute, 1986), p. 189.

18 See C. Shearman, L. Georghiou, M. Gibbons, et al., 'European Collaboration in Liquid Metal Fast Breeder Reactor Research and

Development', report prepared for the European Commission and
Fast Reactor Coordinating Committee, 1986.

*Chapter 3*

1 Christopher Layton, 'The High-Tech Triangle', in Roger Morgan and
Caroline Bray (eds), *Partners and Rivals in Western Europe: Britain,
France and Germany* (Aldershot, Gower for the Policy Studies
Institute, 1986), p. 193.
2 Helen Wallace, with Adam Ridley, *Europe: The Challenge of Diversity*, Chatham House Paper no. 29 (London, Routledge & Kegan Paul
for the Royal Institute of International Affairs, 1985).
3 Layton, 'The High-Tech Triangle', p. 194.
4 House of Lords Select Committee on the European Communities,
*Esprit* (European Research and Development in Information Technology), Session 1984–5, 8th Report (London, HMSO, 1985), p. 169.
5 Ibid., p. 35.
6 For a useful summary of Esprit Phase 1 documentation, see the
European Commission's publication 'Official Documents on the Esprit
Programme', COM (84) 608 (Brussels, Commission of the European
Communities, 1984). For details on Phase 2, see COM (86) 269 final.
7 A full list of Esprit projects can be obtained from the Commission of
the European Communities Task Force for Information Technologies
and Telecommunications, rue de la Loi 200, B-1049 Brussels, Belgium.
8 See Communication from the Commission to the Council and the
Parliament Concerning a Review to Assess the Initial Results of the
Programme Esprit, COM (85) 616 final.
9 ISDN allows voice, data, text and video to be carried. IBCN
represents a higher capacity network which will evolve from and
ultimately subsume the present services and network structures of, for
example, ISDN, cable TV and mobile communications.
10 See, for example, Proposal for a Council Decision on a Preparatory
Action for a Community R&D Programme in the Field of Telecommunications Technologies: R&D in Advanced Communications Technologies for Europe (Race) – Definition Phase, COM (85) 113 final;
and Report of the Commission to the Council on R&D Requirements
in Telecommunications Technologies as Contribution to the Preparation of the R&D Programme Race, COM (85) 145 final.
11 Proposal for a Council Regulation Instituting a Community Programme for the Development of Certain Less-favoured Regions of the
Community by Improving Access to Advanced Telecommunications
Services (Star Programme), COM (85) 836 final.
12 Esprit Information Exchange System, *IES News*, no. 4 (June 1986),
pp. 3–6.

13 For further information, see the European Commission Press Release IP (86) 50 of 4 February 1986, and the Brite Information Package available from DG XII.

14 For a summary of Comett, see *Science in Parliament*, vol. 43 (1985), no. 182. Information on Rare can be obtained from the Rare Secretariat, De Boelelaan 873, 1082 RW, Amsterdam, The Netherlands. See also Esprit Information Exchange System, *IES News*, no. 4 (June 1986), pp. 10–12, and no. 5 (August 1986), p. 4.

15 Initial responses of the West German government to the Brite programme, for example, were lukewarm, but pressure from the German companies involved has resulted in a more enthusiastic approach.

16 The Commission defines SMEs as firms of 500 employees or under, but for many companies, especially in IT, 20 or 30 employees is a large number.

## Chapter 4

1 Commission Memorandum, 'Towards a European Technology Community', COM (85) 350 final (Brussels, Commission of the European Communities, 1985). See also Implementation of the Commission's Memorandum 'Towards a European Technology Community', COM (85) 530 final.

2 For details of the Single European Act, see *Bulletin of the European Communities*, Supplement 2/86.

3 'Eurêka: la renaissance technologique de l'Europe' (Paris, Centre d'Etude des Systèmes et des Technologies Avancés, June 1985).

4 Declaration of Principles Relating to Eureka adopted at Hanover, 6 November 1985.

5 See European Parliament Report, drawn up on behalf of the Committee on Energy, Research and Technology, on the proposal to establish a European Research Coordinating Agency (Eureka), Rapporteur – Mr Glyn Ford, PE 103/286 final (Luxembourg, European Parliament, 1986).

6 For an appraisal of those involving British firms, see Brian Bayliss and Andrew Millington, 'Cross-frontier Joint Ventures and UK Industrial Development', Report of an ESRC research project, ESRC F0023/2008 (London, Economic and Social Research Council, June 1986).

7 'Venture Capital in Europe 1985: Survey on Venture Capital in the European Community', undertaken for the European Venture Capital Association by Peat Marwick Mitchell & Co., EUR 10224 (1985), p. 4.

8 Ibid., p. 37.

9 For further details of all these schemes, see René Guth, 'Initiatives communautaires pour la promotion du capital à risques', *Eurepargne*, no. 7 (July 1986).

10 For example, the deal between Siemens and Toshiba for a licence on the latter's one-million-bit chip technology. See *The Guardian*, 11 February 1986, p. 25.

11 *The Financial Times*, 22 November 1985.

12 J. Patrick Raines, 'Common Market competition policy: the EC-IBM settlement', *Journal of Common Market Studies*, vol. 24, no. 2 (December 1985).

13 Communication from the Commission to the Council, 'The Second Phase of Esprit', COM (86) 269 final.

*Chapter 5*

1 This comment was made at a conference on Europe's technological future organized by the Aspen Institute, Berlin, in October 1986. It was a sentiment echoed by other industrialists around the table.

2 See 'How Europe can fight the multinationals', Michael Butler, *The Financial Times*, 2 February 1986, p. 21.

3 Quoted in an article by Joseph Fitchett in the *International Herald Tribune*, 19 December 1985, pp. 1 and 7, entitled 'Battle of the US titans hastens Europe's technological revolution'.

4 Joan Pearce and John Sutton, with Roy Batchelor, *Protection and Industrial Policy in Europe* (London, Routledge & Kegan Paul for the Royal Institute of International Affairs, 1986), p. 198.

5 The 'general theory of the second best' in economics applies to situations in which some insuperable constraint prevents the achievement of Pareto optimality conditions. Effectively it is a theory about constrained optima, and its most widely applicable result is to show that if perfect competition is not achievable in one sector of the economy, then striving to achieve perfect competition in all other sectors is not, from a general equilibrium point of view, the optimal solution. See R.G. Lipsey and K. Lancaster, 'The general theory of second best', *Review of Economic Studies*, vol. 24 (1956–7), pp. 11–32.

6 See article by Guy de Jonquières, 'Reagan's technology export curbs cut US electronics sales', *The Financial Times*, 16 October 1986.

7 In fact it is a moot point that Europe gained technology or management skills from the US multinationals. It can be argued that much of the technology exploited in the postwar era – the jet engine, nuclear power, space technology, hydrocarbon chemistry – came from Europe; what Europe learnt from the USA was how to exploit these technologies for the benefit of the mass consumer. This is not, however, true of microelectronics, where the seminal breakthroughs in

science have come from US laboratories and firms, although, perhaps ironically, it is the Japanese who are showing the Americans how to exploit these technologies in civilian use. See Margaret Sharp, ed., *Europe and the New Technologies* (London, Pinter, 1985), ch. 8.

8  Kevin Cahill in his book *Trade Wars* (London, W.H. Allen, 1986) argues vehemently that European governments, and particularly the UK, have abjectly bowed to US interests on this issue and as a consequence have allowed European firms to be substantially disadvantaged *vis-à-vis* their US competitors.

9  This theme (i.e., the new toughness of the USA towards Japanese competitors in high technology) is explored at some length by Nicholas Valéry in 'The Clash of the Titans' (High Technology Survey), *The Economist*, 23 August 1986, pp. 11–20.

10  There was sharp comment on this issue in two recent leaders in *The Financial Times*: 'No way to open markets', 13 October 1986; and 'EEC barriers to high technology', 12 January 1986.

11  H. Ergas, *Does Technology Policy Matter?*, CEPS Papers no. 29 (Brussels, Centre for European Policy Studies, 1986).

12  J. Horn, H. Klodt and C. Saunders, 'Advanced Machine Tools: Production Diffusion and Trade', in Margaret Sharp, ed., *Europe and the New Technologies* (London, Frances Pinter, 1985).

# THE AUTHORS

**Margaret Sharp** is a Senior Research Fellow at the Science Policy Research Unit, University of Sussex. Recent publications of hers include *Europe and the New Technologies* (Frances Pinter, 1985) and *The New Biotechnology: European Governments in Search of a Strategy* (Science Policy Research Unit, 1985). She also co-authored an earlier Chatham House Paper with Michael Brech on *Inward Investment: Policy Options for the United Kingdom* (1984).

**Claire Shearman** is currently a Research Associate at the University of Lancaster, having moved there from the Department of Science and Technology Policy at Manchester University. Her work on European collaboration in technology has focused in particular on the fast breeder reactor, computing and telecommunications sectors.